Create THE Perfect FIT

MEASURING AND PATTERN FITTING FOR REAL SEWING SOLUTIONS

Joi Mahon

Fons&Porter

CINCINNATI, OHIO

Table of Contents

Introduction   4

Chapter 1
Measuring and Pattern Protocol   6
› Tools and Supplies   8
› Tips and Tricks for Perfect Measuring   9
› Solving Fit Issues From the Start   10
› Measure Yourself, Measure Your Pattern   12

Chapter 2
Vertical Torso Adjustments   14
› Vertical Torso Measurement Chart   15
› Shoulder to Apex   16
› Bust Curve   18
› Underbust to Waist   21
› Shoulder to Full Back   22
› Back Neck to Waist   23
› Truing Armholes   24
› Vertical Combination Adjustments   26
› Truing Side Seams   27

Chapter 3
Horizontal Torso Adjustments   28
› Horizontal Torso Measurement Chart   29
› Full Bust, Full Underbust and Full Waist   30
› Apex to Apex   31
› Apex to Side Seam   33
› Front Waist   35
› Upper Chest   37
› Center Front Waist to Lower Vertical Bustline   38
› Full Upper Back (Shoulders)   40
› Mid Back (Back Full Bust)   42
› Back Waist   43
› Other Back Pattern Adjustments   44
› Other Horizontal Torso Pattern Examples   46

Chapter 4
Vertical Lower Body Adjustments   48
› Vertical Lower Body Measurement Chart   49
› Center Front Waist to Hips   50
› Center Front Waist to Abdomen   52
› Center Front Waist to Knee   53
› Side Seam Waist to Hips   54
› Center Back Waist to Hips   56

› Vertical Lower Body Combination Patterns   58
› Tips for Blending the Lower Body Side Seams   59

Chapter 5
Horizontal Lower Body Adjustments   60
› Horizontal Lower Body Measurement Chart   61
› Center Front Waist to Side Seam   62
› Center Back Waist to Side Seam   64
› Center Front Waist to Lower Vertical Bustline   66
› Center Back Waist to Back Vertical Line   68
› Center Front to Side Seam at Abdomen   70
› Center Front to Side Seam at Hips   72
› Center Back to Side Seam at Hips   74
› Horizontal Lower Body Combinations   76
› Applying the Method to Pants   77

Chapter 6
Vertical Arm Adjustments   78
› Vertical Arm Measurement Chart   79
› Shoulder Length: Neck to Shoulder Point   80
› Cap Height: Shoulder Point to Full Bicep   81
› Bicep to Elbow   83
› Elbow to Wrist   84

Chapter 7
Horizontal Arm Adjustments   86
› Horizontal Arm Measurement Chart   87
› Bicep   88
› Back Upper Half Cap   90
› Elbow   92
› Wrist   93
› Combination Sleeves and Sleeve Extras   95

Chapter 8
Ease and the Polished Fit   98
› All About Ease   100
› Sewing a Fit Sample   104
› The Fitting   106

Chapter 9
Garment Application Workbook   110
› Using Your Fit Pattern With a Fashion Pattern   112

Garment Styles

The Boxy Jacket	113
The Classic Blouse	114
Princess Seam Bodice	115
Shorts and Pants	116
A-Line Gored Skirt	117
Princess Line Dress	118
The Princess Coat	119
Everyday Dress	120
The Coat Dress	121
The Ball Gown	122

Chapter 10
Real Bodies, Real Fit

	124
› Same Pattern on Different Bodies	126

Fit Challenges

Grammy V	127
Tammie	128
Julie	129
Morgan	130
Cheryl	131
Carol	132
Patricia	133
Susan	134
Lisa	135
Applying Measurements to Men's Patterns	136

Conclusion	137
Index	138
Resources	140
Acknowledgments	141
About the Author	143

Introduction

The history of my method and how it works

Fit does not have to be complicated or hard. As I teach fit and design around the country, students tell me the same thing over and over: "We buy every fit book, take every class and are never satisfied with the results."

Sewists have fit anxiety; thus, sewists are turned off from sewing garments. This is sad to me because sewing is so rewarding. A sewist should not have to feel that they need a college-size textbook to achieve simple results. I see the same methods taught over and over again. These methods worked on body types fifty years ago, but bodies and fitting needs are different today. I wanted to title this *The Best Fit Book Ever!* or *The Only Fit Book You Will Ever Need!* because a lot of old-school thought and fluff is being taught that is time-consuming and unnecessary.

As I pass along my methods, I see students have amazing and instant results. Why or how, you ask? I approach fit at the beginning and consider the proportion of specific areas of a pattern. I want parts of the pattern to correspond to the same areas on the body. Why make generic pattern adjustments that treat the front like the back or change the entire pattern and create more fitting issues? Here are a few of my favorite examples for you to think about:

> Where is the lengthen or shorten line on most torso patterns? It is close to the hem. What if your body measures long from the shoulder to the bust and you lengthen the front of your pattern by using the line printed on the pattern? You are changing the pattern in the wrong area, creating more fit issues and not solving the original fit problem.

> How about increasing the full waist on a pattern? What if you measure 30" (76.2cm) but your pattern measures 26" (66cm)? Where do you add the 4" (10.2cm)? Most people say to add it at the sides or to divide evenly. What if you divide evenly, but you only need the extra across the front because you have a full tummy? You now have a garment that has extra in some areas and not enough in others, plus uneven side seams. Traditional and generic pattern fitting is just that: generic.

> What if you only use your bust, waist and hip

measurements to select a size? Then you have to cut your fit sample apart, add extra fabric to make it bigger, pin it in other areas, make a new fit sample and start all over. What a process!

> Lastly, I get questions about the infamous full bust adjustment all the time. I call it 101 ways to change a dart, but the truth is, this does not address the location of the breast tissue. I will share how I divide the bust area into four quadrants and address the exact locations where the pattern needs to be adjusted.

As I create patterns for clients whom I never see in person, I simply measure my dress form or flat sloper pattern (whatever I am using), measure specific areas of the pattern and compare them to the individual's measurements of the same area. That tells me exactly what I need to do to that specific area of the pattern.

It's really not difficult. *Measure yourself, then measure your pattern.* If a specific area needs to increase or decrease, I adjust only that area. I treat the front separately from the back. With a quick line of a pencil and a snip of the scissors, I now have an instant adjustment that mimics the body. The pattern is neither too big nor too small, and it eliminates most fitting issues that happen mainly due to proportions. It takes a few more measurements than bust, waist and hips, but not many.

Think of it this way: If you were to draft a pattern from a blank piece of paper, you would measure your body and plot reference points to create a map of your body. You would use your exact measurements and, thus, you would start with a pattern that reflected you, not a pattern that was too small, too big, too short or too long in various areas of the pattern. Most fitting issues begin with a flawed pattern that is out of proportion. I eliminate that from the start, leaving the fitting to the art of fine-tuning and perfecting a garment rather than fussing, cutting, redoing and hair pulling. Who wants that?

If you're still processing my ideas, here's another way to think about it: Have you ever sewn a garment or purchased a garment, put it on and thought, "Oh, it would be perfect if this seam were only a little higher, or the dart laid closer to my hip, or the front did not gap because I need just a little more room between the breasts?" We are addressing these things first because they are proportion issues. The details of the garment or pattern do not mimic your body, so of course you will have fit issues. If you need a little extra between the breasts, you don't add that to the side seams! I see that taught all the time, and it is not good fitting information.

How to use this book

You will learn about various body parts to measure and how to easily increase or decrease the corresponding areas of a pattern. This method works for any body shape, size, style and pattern size. Although I use an adult female model (my good friend Abby) to demonstrate, the process is the same for men's and children's clothing too. It is entirely possible to take any area of any pattern and scale it up or down by any amount. Read through Chapter 1 in its entirety before you begin so you learn some basic tips. After that you can jump

around the pattern adjustments because each adjustment is a lesson in itself.

A note on fitting

Remember, pattern adjustments are *raw* proportion adjustments to fit any pattern to the scale of your body. Always sew a test garment, because you will have to do some fine-tuning to polish your look, but the hard stuff will be taken care of before you sew a single stitch. You may need to make a few temporary changes to armholes and necklines if an adjustment happens to intersect these areas, but you will find them easy to address.

Real people, real garments, real fit issues

Fit issues affect all shapes and sizes, from small to large and everything in between. Every technique I teach directly translates to any size. I wanted to bring it full circle in Chapter 10 by showing real people with various fit issues and explaining how their patterns were adjusted to fit them. I also love Chapter 9, where I walk you through the thought process of applying your measurements to various garments. I use a Vogue 1004 Fitting Shell in the lessons because it is close fitting (allowing us to discuss ease) and helps to demonstrate the process more effectively. This pattern is like a worksheet to help you learn the methods and is not meant to be a final fashion garment. Most people will not wear a fit pattern, so use it as a tool. Or, if you prefer, jump right into any pattern of your choice.

I can sum up the entire book by saying the following: *Measure yourself, measure your pattern.* It's that easy! But for those who want more, read on and enjoy. This truly is my trade secret.

—Joi

Chapter 1

Measuring and Pattern Protocol

You are almost ready to delve into my fitting lessons and trade secrets for perfect fitting garments. Before you begin, this chapter will give you all the guidelines you will need for measuring the body and addressing fitting issues at the beginning of the process. It will also provide you with a list of useful tools and, finally, provide step-by-step instructions for performing the easy pattern adjustments you will soon be mastering. Read this chapter in its entirety to learn all of the foundational skills you will need to proceed in the lessons that follow.

Forget the mind-set where you say, "Well, I have never done it this way," or "This other teacher doesn't do it this way." There are lots of methods. This is not a traditional approach, but it is a real and practical approach. I am sharing what I know works for me and what has made me and so many of my students successful. Plus, it's so easy! So put away your fit anxiety, clear your mind and away we go.

Tools and Supplies

You probably already have everything you need to master the pattern fitting techniques taught throughout this book. If not, the supplies are readily available at most retailers. If you find you want more professional supplies, refer to the Resources list in the back of the book.

> › Measurement charts (from the openers of chapters 2–7)
> › Tape measure
> › 18" (46cm) ruler, French curve and hip curve
> › Adhesive dots (optional, and available in any office supply department)
> › Scotch tape or glue stick
> › Paper scissors, tracing wheel and tracing paper
> › Garment tape, masking tape or narrow painter's tape (optional)
> › Oak tag pattern paper (or a 16" × 20" [40.6cm × 50.8cm] or larger spiral sketch pad or sheets of construction paper, or omit and do your adjustments directly on muslin)
> › Muslin fabric
> › Basic sewing supplies for sewing a fit sample
> › Vogue 1004 Misses' Fitting Shell (or comparable pattern) with the size closest to your bust (not chest)
> › Contouring supplies, such as tailoring shoulder pads, sleeve heads, batting, etc.

A note about the fitting shell pattern: This is a tool to learn the techniques. Think of it like a worksheet. It is a starting point, so it can actually be any size. Imagine taking a size-2 pattern and scaling it up to a 28 or vice versa. It is absolutely possible, but most people will not need such a dramatic adjustment. Some people, however, have vintage patterns that are smaller and want to make them bigger. Now you can. Start with a pattern closest to your bust size (*not* chest size), cut out the pattern and eliminate the pattern guide and envelope because they are not relevant to my method. The Vogue 1004 Fitting Shell best illustrates my techniques, while Chapter 9 illustrates application on any pattern and provides a variety of garment styles.

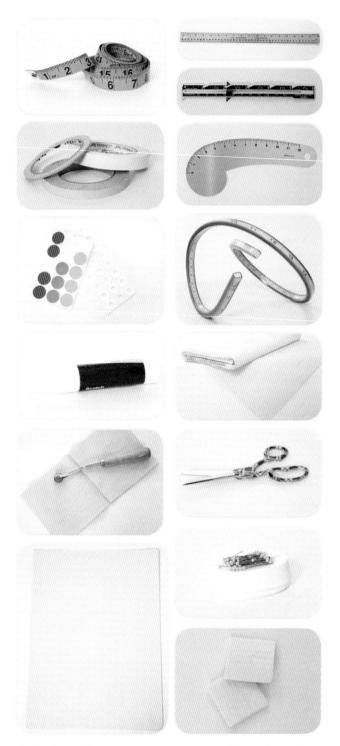

Left column: Tape measure, garment tape, adhesive dots, glue stick, needlepoint tracing wheel and tracing paper (same photo) and oak tag pattern paper.

Right column: 18" (46cm) ruler, hemming gauge, French curve, flexible ruler, muslin, scissors, pins and tailor's chalk.

Tips and Tricks for Perfect Measuring

Sewists of all skill levels have many different ways of doing something as simple as measuring the body. Whatever your method, the most important thing is to be consistent. These numbers will translate to how well your patterns fit. But don't be so literal that you are micromanaging all the numbers. For production, sewing $\frac{1}{32}$ of 1" (2.5cm) is great, but it's okay to round your numbers, if necessary, when customizing your own pattern. Here are a few tips for acquiring your measurements:

› You don't have to be a master tailor to take someone's measurements, but do have someone comfortable with the process take your measurements.

› It is recommended that you do not take your own measurements, but sometimes there's not another option. When taking your own measurements, use adhesive dots to plot key areas where the tape measure needs to start and stop. This will allow for consistency when placing the tape measure on the body. Use garment tape, painter's tape or adhesive tape to map out where you will be measuring. Standing in front of a mirror is helpful as well.

› Be honest with your numbers. We all want a 28" (71.1cm) waist, but just because my pattern measures that does not mean it will fit my body.

› Measure comfortably snug but not tight. A droopy tape measure skews the numbers, but so does a skin-tight tape measure. The tape measure should be close to the body, but you should be able to place one or two fingers between the tape and your body.

› Consider body movement. If you will be sitting, standing, reaching or doing a specific body motion, you may want to measure while doing that motion to allow for movement ease in patterning and, possibly, extra length.

› The body fluctuates and measurements change daily, so don't micromanage your numbers.

› You have permission to round. Don't debate whether a measurement is $\frac{1}{32}$ of 1" (2.5cm). If you want to round to the nearest $\frac{1}{4}$" (6mm) or $\frac{1}{2}$" (1.3cm), that's perfectly fine. There are some checks and balances in the fitting process if you happen to have a little too much wiggle room. I always round up.

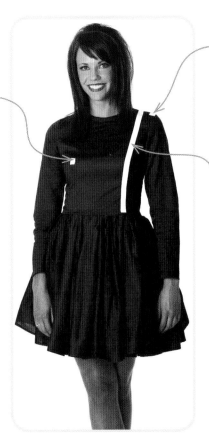

Apex—This is the forward-most point on the breast. On most people, it's the nipple; however, there are times when it is not. The apex is more than a great place to rotate a bust dart or place a design line. This is a key fitting area for the front of the torso, and a starting point for torso adjustments. This is why we do not use chest measurements for selecting a pattern.

Cap shoulder point—This is the point where the arm intersects the shoulder or torso, and it is the placement for the shoulder seam. Ideally, this spot is centered on the arm, but on some individuals it can be recessed back or forward. Because we can't choose our bone structure, you want to be aware of this for fitting sleeves.

Vertical bustline—This is the vertical reference line that extends from the approximate center of the shoulder down to the apex and continues down to the waist and into the lower body. This is *not* the princess seam, which is a design line; however, the princess seam should fall on this line. This line will be your best friend in fit!

A, B, C, the Key 3
Any reference point on the body can be a key measuring point if it is specific to perfecting your fit. As we proceed, treat the front of the body separate from the back and remember that every body is different. If you need further key fitting points besides the apex, the vertical bustline, and the cap shoulder point, add them as necessary.

Solving Fit Issues From the Start

Undergarments

Many fitting issues can be addressed, adjusted and even eliminated by measuring, fitting and wearing the correct underpinnings with your garment. Think of what you are wearing underneath your clothing as a foundation for the garment to rest on. Bad shape underneath equals poor fit on the outside. What are correct undergarments? They might simply be a well fitting bra and full-cut brief (which allows for natural hip curve) or a body shaper, slip and other styling aids. Poorly fitting undergarments create bulges on the outside; they bind into the hip, skew the hip curve and provide little or no support when needed. Professional fitters understand the importance of how this affects final fit. In addition, you will want to address body irregularities and, if possible, camouflage them before you measure and, certainly, before you sew. If you are padding out an uneven shoulder, for example, you do this at the beginning, not at the end.

Asymmetry and figure variations

One leg longer, one hip higher, one shoulder lower and uneven breasts are just a few body dynamics that are common to all ages, shapes and sizes. Some variations are subtle, but some individuals have obvious differences, resulting in major fitting challenges. You probably are thinking of yours right now. Sewists often fit to the defect, forcing two odd-shaped pattern pieces to make an odd-shaped seam or garment that is an exact translation of a figure variation. This is difficult to sew and can challenge even the most expert fitter and sewist. An impossible shape can also mean an impossible fit, creating what I call fit anxiety. You have to think about what you are asking your pattern to do when sewing it into a garment. Textbook-sewn clothing might be perfectly sewn, but if you're walking around with a shoulder 3" (7.6cm) lower than the other, for example, this is not good fit, even if you have applied the most couture methods. Instead, why not contour the body to a more natural shape and easily sew garments with that same natural shape as well? After all, that is what the professionals and true experts in fit do, and you can too!

One style does not fit all. Select the foundation garment that works best with your garment. Shown above: Push up, halter, demi cup, full cup underwire, long line with plunging neck, and strapless.

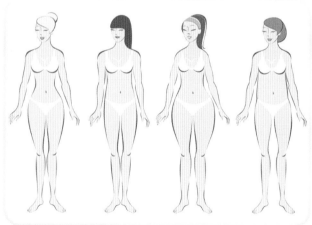

Hourglass, rectangle, pear and inverted triangle are a few of the body silhouettes that illustrate different body types.

Contouring the body

Contouring the body is an easy technique to camouflage unevenness in the body by padding areas that do not match on the other side. What you do depends on the type of garment you're making. A T-shirt may not require anything for casual wear. On the other hand, you don't want your perfectly tailored jacket to highlight your uneven shoulders or protruding hip bone.

Disclaimer: Some extreme cases cannot be completely hidden. A size 20 won't look like a size 4, and if your chin is touching your navel, even the straightest seam will not make you look miles taller. So be reasonable in extreme cases. Here are a few examples of contouring:

- **Uneven shoulder height:** Add height with padding to level out the shorter shoulder.
- **Narrow shoulders:** Extend length with shoulder pads to give a more natural hourglass shape and to avoid making unnecessary narrow pattern adjustments to the upper back or front chest area.
- **Uneven breasts:** Layer bra pads to fill out the smaller side.
- **Saggy breasts:** Give the girls a lift. You can't expect to fit the bust area with droopy girlfriends. A great-fitting bra with support at the shoulders and underneath will change your look, fit and the health of your back. **Note:** For extremely large breasts, consider a longline bra for better lift. This can change your life. It's cheaper than surgery!
- **High hip:** If you have one hip that is higher than the other, create a hip pad by layering shoulder pad materials to raise the lower hip and level out your waist and hipline.
- **Scoliosis:** Contouring a curvature in the spine can be tricky. Sewing padding to a camisole and padding the flat areas can create a flat effect on the back. You can also sew these to the lining.
- **Dowager's hump:** In the case of a severe rounding of the upper back, it may not be ideal to add layers of padding. In this case, we apply our design talents and add beautiful vertical seams to allow for more areas of contour in our garments. A boxy jacket will not lay nice, but princess seams allow for a flattering fit.

Apply body contouring techniques before you measure. This way, you will start the measuring and fitting process with a more polished figure and save time and fitting anxiety. You may have different sets of measurements for different garments, so label accordingly.

Note: The pattern adjustment chapters assume you have measured over correctly fitting undergarments and have addressed major fit issues first.

Dress form designing

Many of my students ask me about using a dress form. I love dress forms. They are like 3-D versions of a commercial pattern, and they, too, are created according to general sizes. They are not custom any more than a pattern is custom right out of the envelope, but they are wonderful tools. I have them in all shapes and sizes. You can contour your dress form to mimic your shape and have your own base for fitting and making your garments. Pad the form where needed and cover it with a swimsuit or tight T-shirt for a fashionable cover.

Contouring materials

Contouring materials include but are not limited to:

- *Seamless bra cups*
- *Clearance bras taken apart for components*
- *Thin but good quality quilt batting sewn in layers with graded edges*
- *Body shapers*
- *Shoulder pads*
- *Tailoring supplies*
- *Interlinings*

Measure Yourself, Measure Your Pattern

Each measurement on the body corresponds to a single area of fit and a single pattern adjustment. In my process, an adjustment or pattern alteration is a *raw* vertical or horizontal increase or decrease of a specific area on the pattern that allows it to replicate the proportion of that same area of your body. A pattern adjusted this way will fit all areas on the body and only needs fine-tuning during the fitting process. Forget having to cut apart areas that are too small or too tight, or allowing for additional time and fit samples.

› Treat the front of the body separately from the back.
› Horizontal measurements have horizontal changes to your pattern.
› Vertical measurements have vertical changes to your pattern.
› You won't need every adjustment provided.
› Address the fullest body contours first.
› Adjustments are either an increase or a decrease.
› Adjustments are *raw* proportion changes.
› Adjustments may intersect and temporarily change an armhole or neckline. Don't get hung up on this. There are tips to explain how to handle this and how to tweak it in the fitting.
› Adjust vertically, then horizontally.

The adjustment process

The process for adjusting your pattern is quick and efficient. You are making *raw* proportional changes to create a pattern that reflects your body shape. After trying this process on a few patterns, you will see your sewing and fitting life change dramatically. The following process can be done on any part of any pattern, even those not listed, and will be the method used on each example throughout this book. I develop new areas of adjustment all the time, and you can, too.

1. Measure yourself, measure your pattern. Measure a segment of your body. Measure that same part of the pattern and compare the two measurements. If they are the same, do nothing. If the pattern is smaller than your body measurement, then you need to increase the pattern to match your body. If the pattern is bigger than your body measurement, decrease that area of the pattern. Body measurement charts are provided in each chapter; however, as you perfect this technique, I encourage you to develop your own custom points of measure unique to your body.

2. Slash and spread. (Figure 1) Using your ruler, draw a cutting line on your pattern within the area to be adjusted. On vertical changes, do not add to the edge of an area. It is always best to slash within the area or approximately in the center. In the example, the red line indicates the shoulder-to-apex measurement. This pattern needed to be made longer for the wearer. You can see that approximately in the middle of this area is where the pattern was spread. The pink area indicates the new addition, and it is also marked with an arrow showing an increase vertically, making the red line or place of measure longer. This process also applies to decreasing a pattern.

3. Truing. (Figures 2 and 3) As you modify your pattern, some design elements will need a little perfecting. Darts are common fitting elements that need to be trued up. Use your ruler to connect the point of the dart to the fat ends of the darts. Things will change within the center of the dart as you change the proportion of your pattern to be either larger or smaller. This is normal. Simply connect the dots after you have made your adjustment. The red line shows where we have trued the darts in the examples. **_Note:_** If you have very large changes and your darts are altered drastically, the tip of the dart will stay the same. Pin fit the dart to your body to get the correct shape. In these situations, the darts may curve rather than have a harsh straight line from the tip to the ends. Side seams are another area that we will make note of truing up.

Tip

When measuring your pattern, do not include seam allowances, darts, gathers or design details that create fullness in the measurement. Stop measuring at the beginning of the detail and start again at the other side.

Cut off your seam allowances for altering the pattern if that makes it easier. Remember to add it back on after all changes have been made.

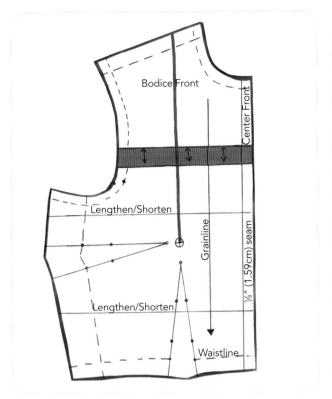

Figure 1

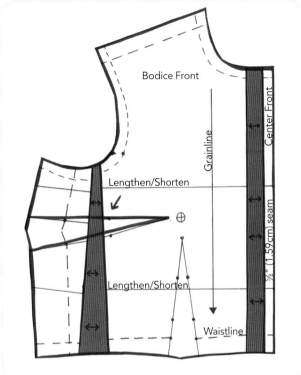

Figure 2

Polishing the fit and the what if's

After you do your raw changes and sew a fit sample, all you have left is polishing the armholes, necklines and minor tweaking. These tasks will be covered in Chapter 8. But what if. . . ? You might be wondering how to make side seams even or, the most common question, what happens if the armhole or neckline changes due to an adjustment. These things are temporary and do not affect the integrity of the method. Throughout the lessons, I will provide solutions if you want to address them immediately at the pattern stage. You can also do what I do and polish up those items in the fit lesson. The choice is yours.

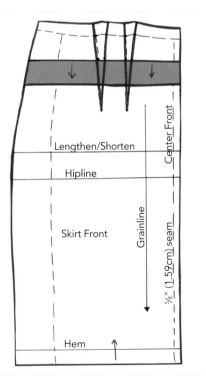

Figure 3

Chapter 2

Vertical Torso Adjustments

If you need to lengthen or shorten a bodice pattern, where do you make the adjustment? Most sewists say near the waist because that is where the pattern has a printed line or where traditional methods have you make the adjustment. But what if you're long from the shoulder to your apex and you lengthen at your waist? You now have a bunchy garment at your waist and a pattern that is still too short toward the top. This example might be new to some and obvious to others, but here is where it gets good. I divide the length of the bodice pattern into three sections called the vertical bustline. I also developed the bust curve adjustment, and I have never seen this taught before. This will revolutionize your bust fitting, guaranteed, as we learn about quadrants 1 and 2. Forget 101 ways to adjust a bust dart and all those generic full bust adjustments. They don't take into consideration the placement of the breast tissue, but this measurement does. Let's delve right into the vertical torso.

Vertical Torso Measurement Chart

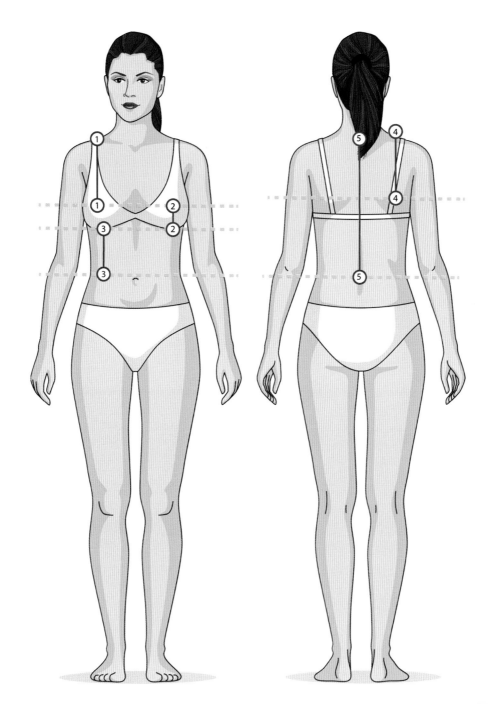

1 Shoulder to Apex	
2 Bust Curve	
3 Underbust to Waist	
4 Shoulder to Full Back	
5 Back Neck to Waist	

Shoulder to Apex

The shoulder-to-apex measurement addresses the upper part of the vertical bustline and how the pattern fits above the apex. It is also helpful to measure from the hollow of the neck to the waist. Although this is not part of the vertical bustline, it can tell you a lot about the length of the upper torso and where changes might need to be made.

> If the shoulder is significantly higher than the hollow of the neck, and you find that you need to increase your upper vertical bustline, make the increase toward the top of your pattern.

> If the shoulder and the hollow of the neck are close to each other, you might need to shorten the upper part of your pattern.

> If the shoulder and the hollow of the neck look average, and you need to shorten or lengthen the upper vertical bustline, you can adjust approximately within the middle of the shoulder-to-apex measurement.

Measure from the approximate center of the shoulder down to the apex, the forward-most point on the bust.

To increase

To increase the upper part of the pattern above the apex, draw a horizontal line across the pattern approximately in the center of the area being measured (the red line, shoulder to apex). Cut and spread the pattern by the amount needed to match your body measurement (no ease included). The arrow indicates increasing the pattern. **Note:** The armhole will temporarily get bigger. This will be addressed at the end of the chapter and does not need to be addressed at this point.

 Locating the Apex on a Pattern

The apex is a key point of measure for pattern making and fit. Patterns normally do not have the apex marked, but it is easy to locate. Draw a line up from the center of the waist dart and over from the center of the bust dart; the intersection is the apex. A good rule is that it is approximately in the center of your pattern.

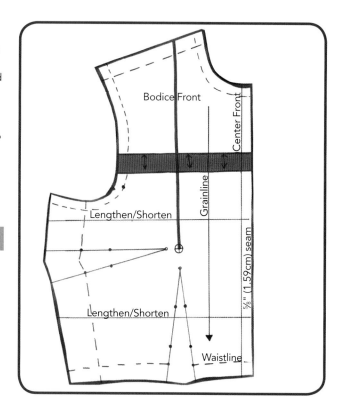

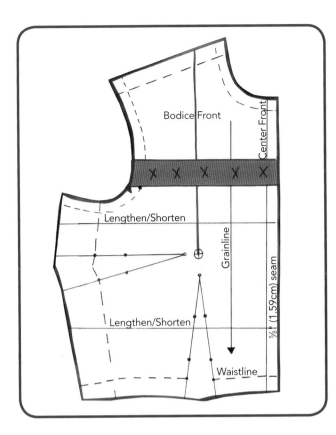

To decrease

To decrease the upper part of the pattern above the apex, draw a horizontal line across the pattern approximately in the center of the area being measured (the red line, shoulder to apex) and cut it apart. Instead of spreading the pattern to add length, overlap one piece over the other, deducting the amount necessary to make the pattern match your measurement. The Xs indicate the portion of the pattern that is being removed.

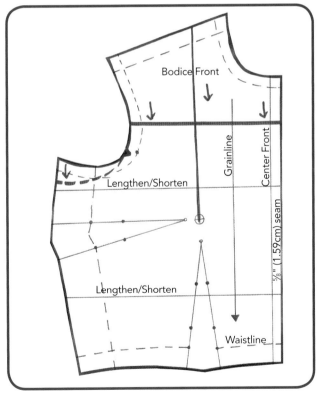

Decrease trued

In this example, the excess pattern has been removed at the horizontal red line, and you can see how the upper part of the pattern is much shorter. *Note:* Truing the armhole will be covered at the end of the chapter, but notice how the armhole was shortened. To get back to the original shape, you simply measure down the side seam by the amount that was deducted and true up with your French curve.

Darts and the Apex

The textbook rule of thumb is that darts angle toward the apex and stop approximately 1" (2.5cm) before the apex. This may vary, but ideally your darts will stop before crossing the apex.

Bust Curve

The bust curve is a vital location for customizing a pattern, no matter what size breasts you have. I have the most to say about this measurement because I have never seen this addressed in any other fitting methods. By targeting where the breast tissue falls (see "Four quadrants" below) in relation to the apex, you can grade your pattern to reflect your true body proportion. This is where those full-bust adjustments simply do not provide fitting solutions for the bust-fitting issues many sewists have.

Consider where the fullness of the breast tissue is. Is it above the apex (quadrant 1) or below (quadrant 2)? Breasts come in all shapes and sizes. Some very full, round breasts might have a short bust curve with their fullness above the apex, while smaller breasts might have a long length below the apex. Of course, the combinations are unlimited.

The bust curve area (below the apex) is *not* marked or printed on any pattern, but there is space on the pattern allocated to this measurement. The number-one question I receive is, where is the bust curve? To illustrate, hold the pattern up to your body. You can tell right away if the pattern has enough vertical length. In my experience, I have found that approximately 2½"–3" (6.4cm–7.6cm) below the apex is the amount a standard B-cup size pattern will provide the wearer.

Measure from the apex downward, following the curvature of the breast and stopping at the underbust line (approximately the placement of your bra band).

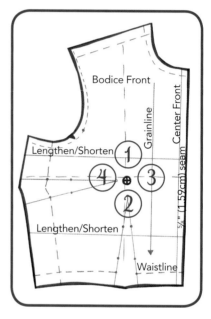

Four quadrants
The four quadrants of the bust area show how different parts of a pattern match the breast for correct fit. Quadrant 2 addresses the bust curve.

 Why adjust this area of the pattern and not just change the bottom since we are below the apex?

Consider what you are asking your pattern and fitting to do. When you lengthen or shorten the bust curve, you're also modifying the part of the pattern directly across from the curve (near the side seam), and this area will need the same proportion as the curve. The lower part of the pattern fits the body differently. The wider part of the waist dart is pulling in more fabric to contour around the waist, which is a different area of fit. If you limit yourself to only adjusting at the bottom of the torso pattern, you are not allowing for change in an area of the body that has its own unique, curved shape.

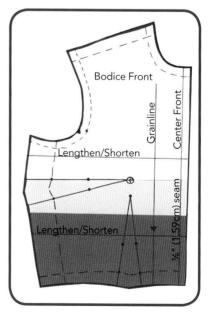

The pale pink section illustrates the area on the pattern that corresponds to the bust curve.

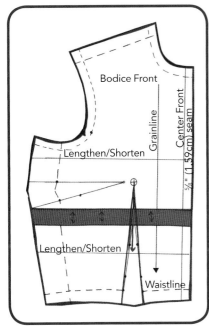

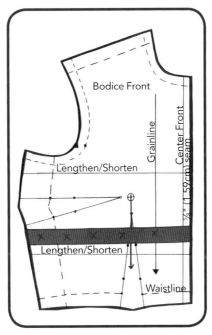

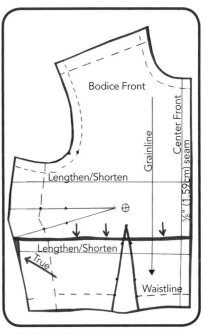

To increase

Measure down 3" (7.6cm) from the apex of your pattern and draw a line horizontally across the pattern. Anything above this line is the bust curve of the pattern. Compare your measurement to this area of the pattern. To increase, simply spread the pattern and add length within the bust curve area on the pattern. True up your darts.

To decrease

Measure down 3" (7.6cm) from the apex and draw a horizontal line across the pattern. Compare your bust curve to the pattern. Cut across the pattern and remove the amount necessary to match your body measurement. The Xs indicate the portion of the pattern that is being removed.

Decrease trued

In this example, the excess has been removed. You can see how the pattern is shorter right below the apex, but the bottom portion of the pattern stayed the same. True up the waist dart and side seam if applicable.

 Tip

The bust curve is somewhat fluid in that there are many ways to apply this adjustment to the pattern. It is still very simple, so don't overthink its application. As you see the benefit of this measurement in particular, you will find that you can further refine its use in your fitting.

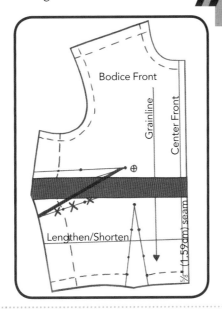

Bust Curve Increase Through the Side Dart

*For large increases in the bust curve, it's best to cut through the dart, causing it to increase. The bigger the curve, the bigger the dart necessary in fitting. **Truing Trick:** When you true the dart after an increase, make sure to line up the ruler from the tip of the dart to the lower edge of the side dart. The dart becomes much bigger, but when sewing your side seams, it stays the same from front to back because, while you are increasing below the apex, you are tapering the pattern back in at the sides. If you do not want to have to true side seams, you can always adjust through the dart if you choose. Experiment with this application, because there are many reasons to use or not use the dart, all with varying results.*

More on the bust curve measurement

The two-piece princess bodice pattern further illustrates the bust curve area of measure. The side front pattern has a prominent "P" shape meant to contour to the shape of the breast. The apex is marked on the pattern and lines up with the apex on your bust area. We know from our lessons in this chapter that the bust curve is the area below the apex down to the underbust line (or bra band line). This pattern has been adjusted and lengthened in the bust curve area as well as the lower vertical bustline. Do you see what happens to the bust curve area when it is lengthened? The corresponding area of the pattern that matches the side seam and the center front is adjusted as well. Often darts and other bust-fitting details fall in these areas. Think about what is going on with the shape of the body in relation to the pattern.

If you only lengthened the lower part of the pattern, you would never adjust all these other key areas of fit. You would only be making the bottom of the pattern longer or shorter.

Different Shapes of the Bust Curve

- *Very full breasts have a longer bust curve on the underside and need an increase.*

- *Smaller breasts may have a short bust curve on the underside and need a decrease.*

- *Breasts with implants might be very large and bulbous on the top, but they could have a shorter or average bust curve underneath. Size may not always determine an adjustment.*

- *Nursing breasts can be all over the place, but an elongated bust curve is common. Adjusting the pattern traditionally does not fit the nursing breast.*

- *Someone with a pronounced chest cavity might have small breasts, but the underbust curve could be longer due to the contour of the body.*

- *Each curve is unique.*

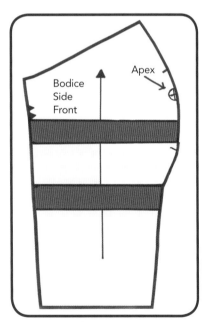

Two-piece bodice side front pattern

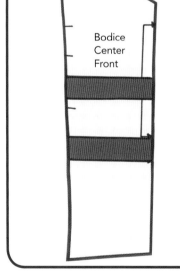

Two-piece bodice center front pattern

The bust curve in the "P"

A two-piece princess bodice patterns really exhibits the location of the bust curve. The distinctive curve of the "P" shape matches the curve of the bust below the apex. Where the pattern straightens out relates to the lower part of the torso, or the underbust to waist (lower vertical bustline), which is discussed on the following page.

Underbust to Waist

Adjustments to lengthen or shorten the length of a bodice or torso pattern are traditionally made in a single adjustment. It is not uncommon to lengthen higher in the pattern and shorten in the lower or vice versa. You might have already caught on that there are reasons to adjust in various places on the vertical bust-line. By dividing the vertical bustline into three sections, you can better refine the fit and make a pattern that more closely reflects your proportion. This third section, the lower vertical bustline, affects the fit in the areas closer to the waist.

This is an area where you can use the printed lengthen/shorten line on your pattern. Remember, you are increasing only the lower part of the pattern below the bust curve. On an unchanged pattern, the bust curve area stops approximately 2½"–3" (6.4cm–7.6cm) below the apex. You will be adjusting between that line and the waist or lower edge of your pattern.

Measure from the underbust (bra band line) down to the natural waist.

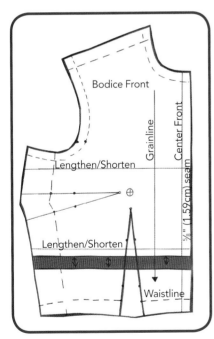

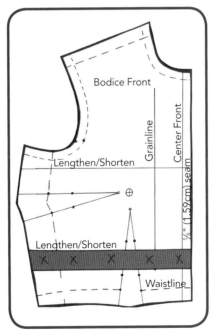

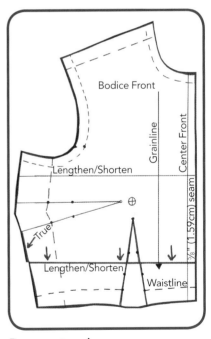

To increase

Draw a horizontal line in the middle of the underbust-to-waist area or use the printed lengthen line. Cut across the line and spread the pattern open to add length to match your body measurement. True up your dart. The arrows indicate increasing.

To decrease

To decrease, draw a horizontal line in the middle of the underbust-to-waist area, or utilize the shorten line printed on the pattern. Cut across your line and remove the amount necessary so your pattern reflects your body measurement. The Xs indicate the portion of the pattern that is being removed. True up your dart.

Decrease trued

In this example of the decrease, the extra pattern length has been removed. The lower part of the pattern has been changed and is shorter. The dart has been trued and is referenced with the red lines. Also, a small amount of truing was needed at the side of the pattern.

Shoulder to Full Back

The upper part of the back torso pattern is one you want to pay special attention to if you are creating tailored jackets, shirts and garments that require sleeve fitting. This is also an area where you might use some of those body-contouring tips and tricks to create a more natural shape because, as we age, the shoulders roll forward, causing more length and fit issues. This is also an important area to consider when sewing for athletes, who tend to be husky in the upper back.

If the fullest part of your back is in line with your underarm, then you can utilize the printed lengthen/shorten line as a reference. If you do not have a line printed, measure down 1" (2.5cm) from the underarm and draw a horizontal line across the pattern. Everything above the line is your upper back.

If the fullest part of your back is above the underarm, and often it is, then visually divide the back pattern into thirds and draw a horizontal line on your pattern indicating the upper third. Everything above the line is your upper back.

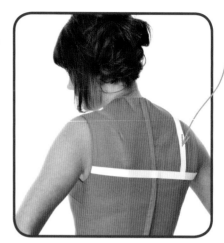

Measure from the center of the shoulder down to the fullest part of the back. This may or may not be the location of your shoulder blades and may or may not line up perfectly with your underarm.

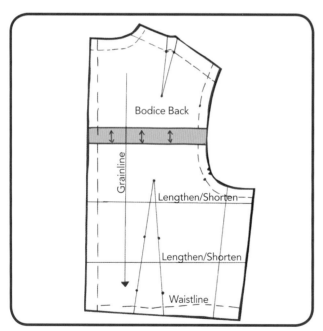

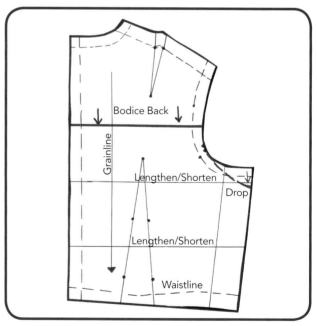

To increase

Measure your shoulder to full back and compare to your pattern. At approximately the center of the upper back area of the pattern, draw a horizontal line across the pattern and cut it apart. Spread the pattern by the amount needed so it is the same length as your upper back measurement. Your armhole will become bigger temporarily. We will address that later in this chapter. For now you can leave it.

To decrease

Measure your shoulder to full back and compare to your pattern. At approximately the center of the upper back area of the pattern, draw a horizontal line across the pattern and cut it apart. Deduct the amount needed to make the pattern match your body measurements. Your armhole will become smaller temporarily. On this example, I have dropped the armhole at the side seam by the amount that we reduced the pattern, putting it back to the original size.

Back Neck to Waist

This is an interesting place of measure on the body. It not only gives you an indication of how long to make your back pattern, but it provides insight to how your clothing will perform on your body due to posture. As I have measured and fitted all types of body shapes and sizes, I have observed certain characteristics with the center back. Dancers tend to stand very erect, so they have a very straight spine. Some people stand with the spine curving forward, creating a hollow at the small of the back. They might have sagging fabric at their waist, which is a common fitting concern. Other issues with the center back include scoliosis and dowager's hump. Don't forget to apply some body contouring, if applicable, to the body before measuring.

Do this adjustment after you have completed the shoulder-to-full-back adjustment because you still might need some extra length at the bottom, or you may need an additional decrease or a combination of the two.

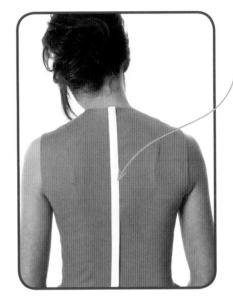

Measure from the neck bone straight down to the natural waist.

The lower part of the back torso pattern is adjusted closer to the waist. Most patterns will have a printed lengthen/shorten line that you can utilize, or you can draw a horizontal line approximately in the middle of the lower pattern.

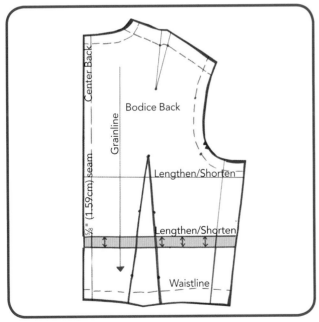

To increase

Measure from the back of the neck to the natural waist. Cut across the pattern on the lengthen line. Spread the pattern by the amount needed so it matches your body measurement. The arrows indicate an increase. True your dart tip to the ends. Notice your side seam now increases. You may or may not have an increase on the front of your pattern. For now, the difference is temporary.

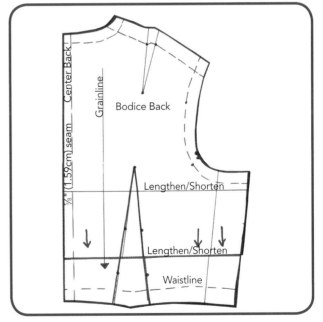

To decrease

Measure from the back of the neck to the natural waist. Cut across the pattern on the shorten line. Overlap or remove the amount needed on the pattern so it becomes shorter to match your body measurement. The pattern is moved downward, reducing the length of the lower pattern. True your dart. Your side seams become shorter. They may or may not match the front pattern, but any difference is temporary.

Truing Armholes

As you lengthen or shorten various areas of the torso pattern, you might have encountered some temporary changes to the armhole, making it either too long or too short. Or are they? Some of these changes will actually translate to some figure types, while others may not. They are temporary, however, and you have a few easy solutions.

If your sewing and design mind-set will let you, these changes can wait to be addressed during the muslin fitting stages. This is what I do, and it allows me to evaluate the armhole visually on the body. In some instances, the shortened or elongated shape did apply to the body. Some students with a traditional mind-set in fit have a hard time with this, but there is a method to my madness. It is not that we are ignoring these changes. We are simply shifting them to another stage of the process for polishing.

To address these issues immediately after a pattern adjustment, use the following information.

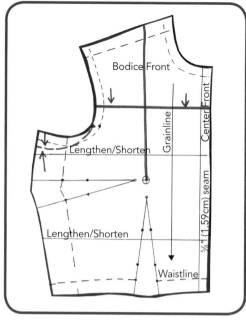

Drop the armhole

If you shorten the upper torso pattern, the armhole will shorten by the same amount (assuming your adjustment intersected the armhole). Take the amount that you decreased the pattern and measure down that same quantity at the side seam, causing it to drop. Use your French curve to true up the shape. Notice that you are back to the original length.

Template

This is a great technique for truing any area of a pattern. Before making any pattern adjustments, trace the edge of your armhole onto a separate piece of paper. Set that aside. Adjust the pattern, then true up your armhole by placing the template over the adjusted pattern. Match the top edge at the shoulder and trace for the original shape. Note: If you have extreme adjustments, you most likely will need to apply some of the changes to the armhole that were made to the pattern. Be reasonable in what you expect in those situations.

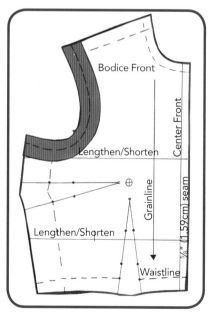

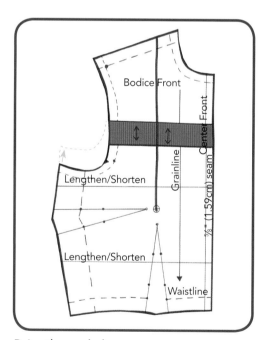

Raise the armhole

If you lengthen the upper torso pattern, the armhole will elongate by the same amount (again, assuming your adjustment intersected the armhole). Take that same amount of increase and draw a line upward at the side seam, raising the armhole or putting it back to the original location. Use your French curve to true up the shape. See how the bodice is longer, but the armhole is back to original size.

Traditional Armhole Method

In custom fitting for individuals, I treat the arm separately from the torso. The traditional method is not my method of choice, but I have many traditional students, so I want to include this example for your reference. It illustrates what you find in many methods for addressing the changes that happen to the armhole after adjusting a torso pattern.

As the front and back torso patterns become longer, or even shorter, you would make that very same adjustment to the sleeve pattern, allowing for the sleeve to match. If the torso is longer, then the sleeve cap becomes longer. If the torso is shortened, then the sleeve cap is shortened. From a flat pattern perspective, or thinking about how industry creates patterns that fit the general population, this would make sense. You need a generic application that meshes the pieces together. What I find in fitting individual bodies, however, is that the generic adjustment to the arm requires more refining, and I am not happy with the outcome.

But if your mind is connecting to this example, then these patterns are for you.

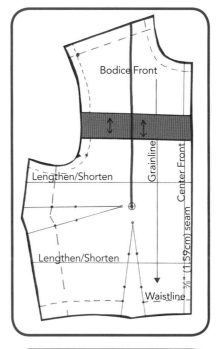

Front adjustment
The front upper torso becomes longer (or shorter).

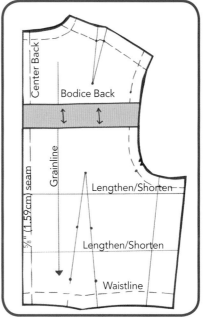

Back adjustment
The back upper torso becomes longer (or shorter).

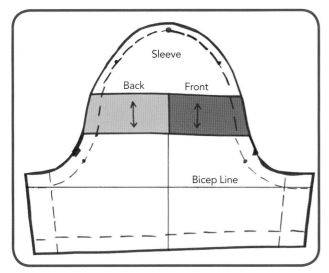

Sleeve cap adjustment
The generic sleeve cap adjustment on a pattern makes it longer (or shorter) in the front and back of the pattern to match the torso patterns. Can you think of a reason this might not work? After studying Chapter 6, return to this page.

Vertical Combination Adjustments

As we have gone through this chapter, we have approached each measurement of the body as a separate area of adjustment. Not every person will need every adjustment, but most people will need a few, and that creates combination patterns. I want you to quickly and efficiently be able to do all your adjust-

ments on the same pattern. Do not make a new pattern after you have completed one adjustment. Move onto the next and polish up the edges at the end.

Here you can see a combination of adjustments on the front and back of a pattern that could easily belong to you, the student.

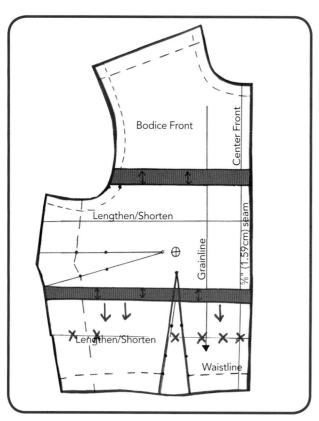

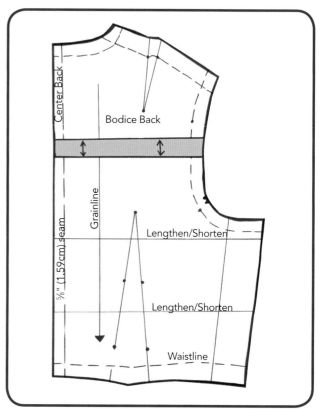

Front combination

This pattern has been lengthened in the upper vertical bustline, lengthened in the bust curve and, interestingly, shortened at the lower vertical bustline (noted by the Xs). A student in one of my classes had this exact pattern. She said that, from a mathematical perspective, the pattern unaltered would be the correct length and fit, but in reality it did not fit at all. So imagine a person who needs these adjustments using only the single preprinted lengthen/shorten line provided on most patterns. It won't work! Other things to note are the armhole becoming longer (that is polished up in the fitting) and the trued dart.

Back combination

This back pattern is the mate to the front combination pattern. What do you notice that is different? Only the upper back has been lengthened, and no other length has been made. By treating the front of the body separately from the back, you gain a better fit. We do have to join the pieces together at the sides, which brings us to the final trick for vertical adjustments: truing the side seams.

Truing Side Seams

In our front combination pattern, we have lengthened the bust curve and shortened the lower vertical bustline. These adjustments balance each other out, resulting in no change of the length of the side seam.

In the process of treating the front separately from the back, however, you might temporarily end up with one side seam longer than the other. Don't get hung up on this or overthink the solution, because it is pretty easy. Simply lengthen the side that is shorter and true it up during the muslin fitting (see Chapter 8).

You might be wondering, if we measured the body, then why would one side be longer than the other? Here is what happens. People are used to seeing patterns that have harsh straight lines. The waist contour from the center back around to the center front is not a harsh straight line. It usually curves, and some people dip in the center front or center back. As we take our measurements for length, we are usually addressing issues closer to the center of the body, so we don't address the contour at the side seam intersection. If we were doing a full pattern draft from scratch, we could address this more in depth. But don't overthink this. Again, we are creating *raw* proportional adjustments to grade our pattern, and we can polish up these areas later in the muslin fitting.

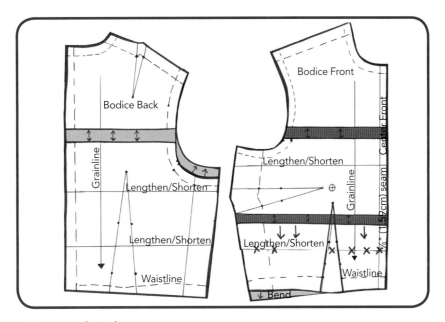

Compare the side seams
Bring the side seams together and compare any difference. Start by matching the top of the side seam and work downward. Extend any side that is too short. You may also need to add length at the top if major armhole changes were necessary. In the fitting stage, you will determine the final and exact waist and armhole shape.

Horizontal Torso Adjustments

If you have a waist that measures 36" (91cm), but your pattern measures 30" (76cm), where would you add the extra 6" (15cm) to make the pattern fit? I always ask this question in my classes, and my students usually reply with one of the following: at the side seams, divide evenly among all the seams, or let out or take in the darts and seam allowance. All of these are incorrect. These all assume the body is perfectly symmetrical, among other reasons. Years ago, when women were smaller and corsets graced our bodies, a generic side seam adjustment would be sufficient; however, the modern body has many more fitting issues.

So if we can't add evenly to all the side seams, let's explore how horizontal measurements can be customized to fit the contours of the figure.

Horizontal Torso Measurement Chart

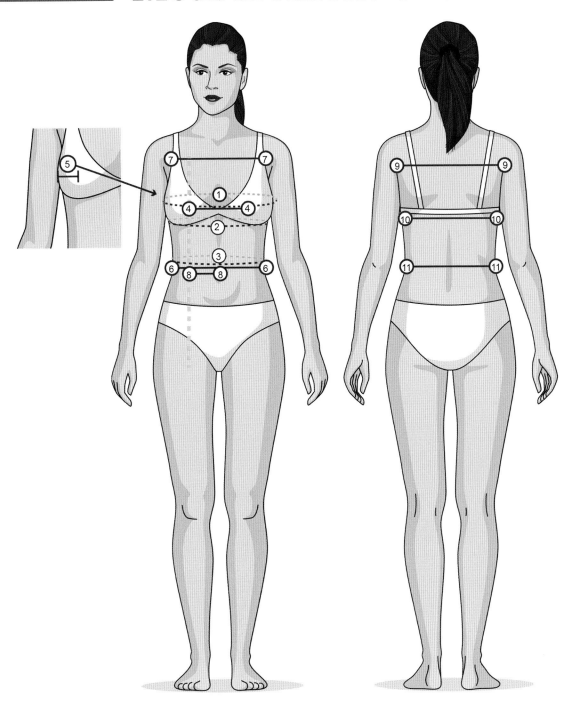

1	Full Bust	
2	Full Underbust	
3	Full Waist	
4	Apex to Apex	
5	Apex to Side Seam	
6	Front Waist	
7	Upper Chest	
8	Center Front Waist to Lower Vertical Bustline	
9	Full Upper Back (Shoulders)	
10	Mid Back (Back Full Bust)	
11	Back Waist	

Full Bust, Full Underbust and Full Waist

Full circular measurements are not customized enough to refine the fit of your pattern. A lot of fit information being taught today has you use only the full bust, waist and hip measurements, and it has you add or subtract only at the side seams to make generic adjustments. Sometimes they have you divide any changes among every seam evenly around the garment. This works to give you volume, but it does not necessarily put the adjustments in the correct locations. What happens if you are wider across the front, but you add evenly at the side seams? You now have too much fabric in the back and not enough in the front. This creates new fit issues, such as side seams that angle in one direction because one side is too short and is pulling for extra fabric.

You cannot make a generic total increase or decrease on a pattern and expect a great fit. So how do you use the full circular measurements? The full total circular measurements provide great checks and balances for the following measurement lessons. As you divide the body into smaller, more customizable areas, logic will tell you that adding up the smaller areas will total the full measurement. It also gives you a starting point for selecting a pattern size.

Remember that the full circular measurements are for totals only. Treat the front of the pattern separately from the back when you want to master your measurements and pattern.

Full bust: Measure over the fullest part of the bust while wearing correctly fitted undergarments.

Full underbust: Measure around the body at the location of your bra band or at the base of the bust curve. This usually falls along the rib cage, but it can vary.

Full waist: Measure around your natural waist. The natural waist is not the location where you wear your low-cut pants. For fit patterns, find the location where the body contours at the hip. Bend slightly to the side with your hands on your hips or place a piece of elastic around your waist and find the natural location.

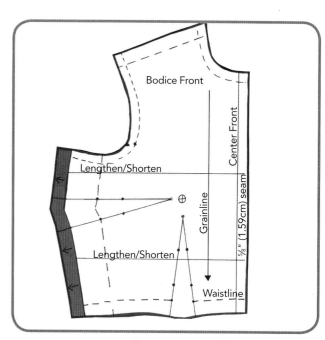

Pattern with side-seam-only adjustment.

Apex to Apex

The apex is a key point of measure for pattern making and fit. Patterns normally do not have the apex marked, but it is simple to locate. Draw a line up from the center of the waist dart and over from the center of the bust dart. This intersection is the apex. For patterns that do not have these darts, a good rule of thumb is that the apex is approximately in the center of your pattern, or half way between the center front and side seam and half way down from the shoulder to the waist. You can also pin your pattern to a dress form and mark the approximate location. You know it is not up by the shoulder, down at the waist or at the center front or side seam. Knowing that, you can logically make a visual decision where it is on the pattern. Don't overthink its placement. It is a starting point for customizing your pattern, and the entire pattern will change around it.

The apex-to-apex pattern adjustments are the easiest to make, yet they are key to perfecting the fit of your garments. This area not only affects whether the center front of a garment will gap open, but it also grades the center front area of the bust measurement (quadrant 3 in bust fitting). **Note:** The pattern examples here are half of a symmetrical pattern. You will use half of your apex-to-apex measurement.

Measure from one apex (forward-most bust point) across the center front to the other apex.

Modifying Measurements

After you master your measurements and see how they relate to your pattern, you have the freedom to intentionally create artificial points on the body by modifying the measurements. For example, if your bust area is narrow, and you want it to look wider, make your apex-to-apex measurement wider. Do the opposite if you want to make the center front look narrow. The body does not change, but you can affect how it's perceived visually.

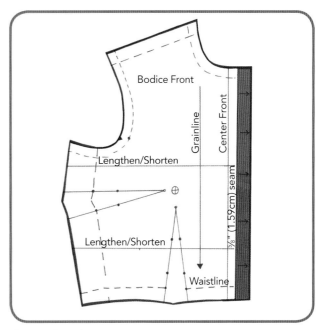

Center front increase
Measure from the apex of the pattern to the center front of the pattern. Do not include the seam allowance. Compare this measurement to half of your body's apex-to-apex measurement. To increase, simply extend the center front of the pattern by the amount needed to match. (The center front neckline will temporarily become longer. You may need this, or you can pin this out in the muslin fitting stage.)

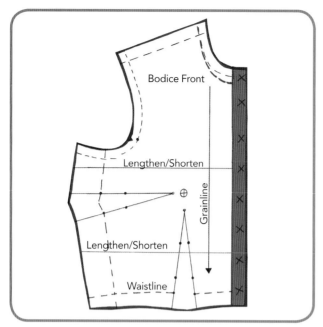

Center front decrease

Measure from the apex of the pattern to the center front of the pattern. Do not include the seam allowance. Compare the measurement to half of your body's apex-to-apex measurement. To decrease, simply deduct from the center front of the pattern the amount needed to match. The Xs indicate the portion of the pattern that is being removed. (The center front neckline will temporarily become narrower. You can clip this open in the muslin fitting or drop the center front neckline by the amount you reduced the pattern. This is noted with the red dotted line.)

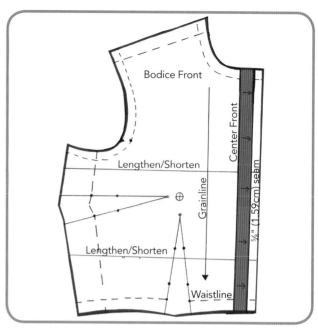

Center front slash increase

If you have a design detail, or a reason not to increase the apex-to-apex distance right on the edge of the pattern, you can slash and spread without interrupting the center front. Measure in approximately 1" (2.5cm) and cut up through the pattern. Spread and increase evenly.

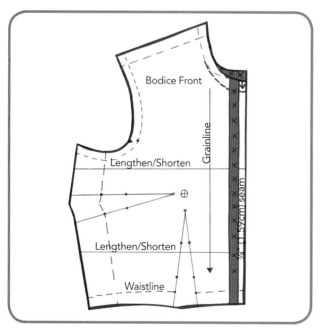

Center front slash decrease

If you have a design detail or a reason not to decrease the pattern right along the edge, you can slash and decrease within the body of the pattern. Be careful not to do this too far into the pattern. Measure over approximately 1" (2.5cm) and cut up through the pattern. Decrease the amount necessary. The Xs indicate the portion of the pattern that is being removed. Note the optional neckline adjustment. Because the reduction makes the neckline narrower, you can measure down at the center front and open it back up. You can also omit this and clip it open during the fitting stage.

Apex to Side Seam

This measurement will give you the length of the bust area on the side (quadrant 4 in bust fitting), which can vary greatly from person to person. This fourth quadrant for addressing how to fit the bust is another reason why traditional full-bust adjustments do not truly customize the bust.

Patterns such as a two-piece princess bodice will have a side front and a center front pattern. The side front piece will match the apex-to-side-seam measurement. This is also why using only the total bust measurement is not a good idea. You need to have the side front of your pattern match your body.

We will utilize the side seam for increasing or decreasing the front torso pattern, but we are only addressing the front of the body and making the pattern match that side front area.

Measure from the apex (forward-most bust point) to the side seam.

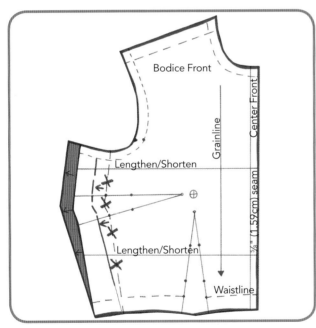

Side seam increase

Measure from the apex to the side seam on the pattern (you can measure straight across the top of the dart if necessary) and compare this measurement to your body measurement. If you need to increase the distance, measure out from the side seam and add the needed width. True your side seam and taper to nothing at the waist. You may need to adjust the waist later, but for this example we are only addressing the side seam to the apex. This fit pattern has a nice 2" (5.1cm) seam allowance, and the stitching line has now shifted outward as noted by the new dotted line. Marking this is optional.

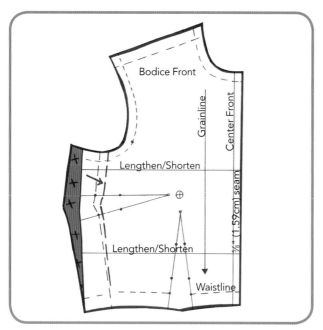

Side seam decrease

Measure from the apex to the side seam on the pattern and compare this measurement to your body measurement. If you need to decrease the width of the pattern, measure inward and create a reduction. The Xs indicate the portion of the pattern that is being removed. True your side seam and taper down to the waist. The fit pattern still has a nice 2" (5.1cm) seam allowance. The stitching line has shifted inward as noted by the dotted line.

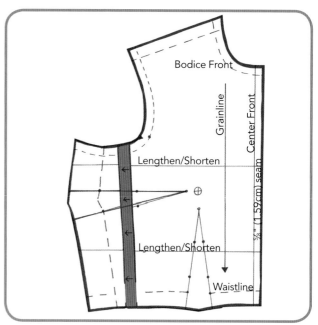

Slash-and-spread increase

If you have a reason to keep the integrity of the side seams, you can increase the distance of the apex to the side seam by doing a slash-and-spread. Measure in from the side seam about 1" (2.5cm) (not including the seam allowance), cut up through the pattern and spread the needed amount to match your body. *Note:* This will temporarily modify the armhole (see the armhole solutions in Chapter 2). Also note that you cannot taper down to the waist. By doing this slash-and-spread, you are also increasing the waist and adjusting two areas. True your dart.

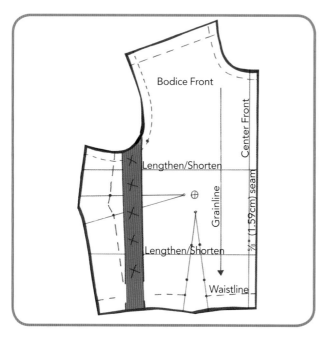

Slash-and-spread decrease

You can decrease this area of measure using the slash-and-spread method. Measure in from the side seam about 1" (2.5cm) (not including the seam allowance), cut up through the pattern and remove the amount needed to decrease the distance from the apex to side. The Xs indicate the portion of the pattern that is being removed. Again, by doing the slash-and-spread, you will affect the waist and decrease there as well. *Note:* The armhole will temporarily become narrower. You can clip it open in the fitting stage or see armhole solutions in Chapter 2.

Front Waist

The front waist measurement is a useful measurement for dividing that full waist into more customizable sections. By treating the front separately, you can really address the contour of the midsection. Most people are wider across the front than the back. Have you ever had a side seam that was not straight up and down? It is possible that the pattern was too wide across the back and not wide enough across the front. This measurement will address those issues.

Width adjustments like the front waist should not be made by taking in or letting out the seam allowance or things like darts and gathers, but that is often what people do. These adjustments need to happen within the body of the pattern or on an edge of the pattern.

Measure from the side seam at the waist across the front of the body, to the other side seam. *Tip:* Use garment tape to place a vertical side seam on the body. This will allow you to start and stop at the same location when you measure the back section.

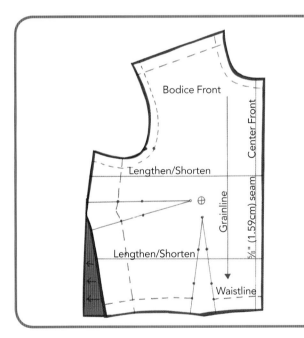

Side seam increase

This is one pattern change where you can use the side edge for the adjustment, but you are only addressing the front body measurement on the front of the pattern. Measure from the center front waist of the pattern over to the side seam. Do not include darts or things like gathers or other design details in this measurement. If you come to a dart, stop your tape measure, jump over the dart and resume measuring until you reach the side seam (do not include the seam allowance). Extend the waist outward by the amount needed. True up your side seam and taper to nothing as you straighten the side.

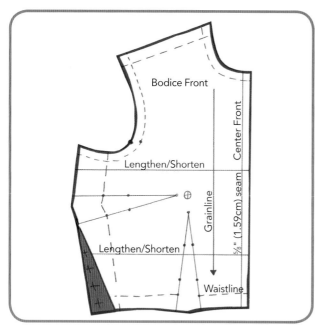

Side seam decrease

You can decrease the waist only on the edge of the pattern. Measure from the center front of the pattern over to the side seam. Do not include darts or other design details. If you come to a dart, stop the tape measure, jump over the dart and resume measuring until you reach the side seam (do not include the seam allowance). Measure inward on the waist and decrease by the amount needed to match your measurement. True up your side seam. The Xs indicate the portion of the pattern that is being removed.

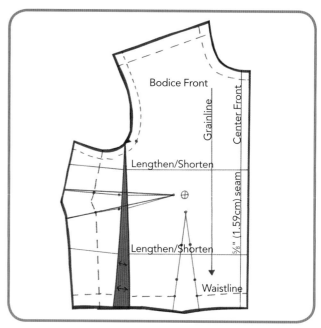

Slash-and-spread increase

The slash-and-spread increase works on the waist if you want to keep the integrity of the side seam. Not including the seam allowance, measure in approximately 1" (2.5cm) at the waist and slash up vertically on your pattern. Cut to, but not through, the edge of your pattern. This will create a hinge. Shift the pattern open at the waist by the amount needed to match your measurement. True the dart that was intersected. *Note:* This does add a small amount to the apex-to-side-seam area.

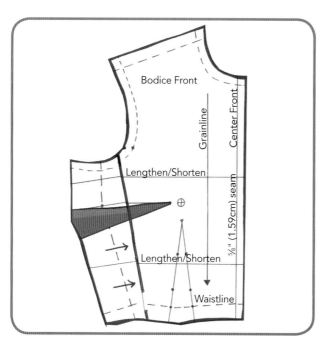

Slash-and-spread decrease

To decrease using the slash-and-spread method, follow the same process. Slash up vertically on your pattern approximately 1" (2.5cm) in from the side seam. Cut up to, but not through, the edge of the pattern. Shift the pattern inward to decrease the waist. This will slightly decrease the apex to side seam, and you will need to true up the dart. This is a really clean adjustment to the waist.

Upper Chest

The upper chest area of a pattern is a common area to adjust. Many people have narrow upper torsos and find that patterns are baggy or too long. My application of the L-slash to this area is perfect if you have this fitting issue.

The L-slash is an adjustment traditionally applied to a sleeve pattern. I have found that you can apply this to an area that you need to adjust without affecting other parts of the pattern.

Measure across the chest (above the full bust) from one armhole to the other. *Tip:* Use garment tape to create an armhole line for ease in measuring.

Contorting vs. Contouring

Remember, don't fit to the defect. Rather than contorting patterns, you might be better off contouring the body. If you are tailoring a jacket or making a blouse, you might want to add some length to the shoulder and pad out a hollow upper chest to create a more natural armhole and seam line. Sometimes as much as ½" (1.3cm) makes all the difference. Also, if you are fuller in the waist or hips, extending these lines will help balance out the body.

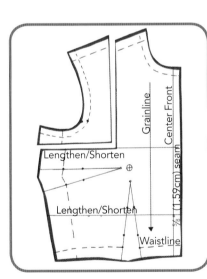

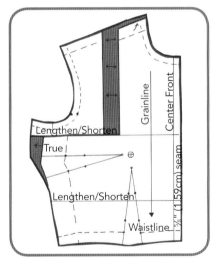

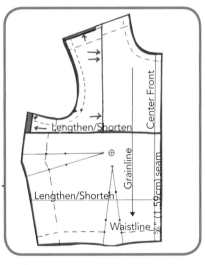

L-slash

On the upper chest, we need to create a pattern segment that can be shifted inward or outward. Above the bust dart, draw a horizontal line across the pattern. You can use the printed lengthen/shorten line for this adjustment. Otherwise, find the approximate center between the armhole and the top of the bust dart. Draw a vertical line from the approximate center of the shoulder to the horizontal line. Cut on these lines, removing the upper portion of the pattern. You now have a movable section of pattern.

To increase

After slashing your segment of pattern, shift it outward by the amount needed to increase the upper chest to match your body measurement. True up any area (such as the side seams) where there is a small gap, as well as the upper shoulder. Notice that the adjustment changes the upper part of the pattern but not the lower part of the pattern. This is great for those who have a fuller upper torso.

To decrease

After slashing your segment of pattern, shift it inward to decrease the upper chest to match your body measurement. True up any area, such as the outer shoulder and the upper edge of the side seam. Notice that the adjustment has changed the upper part of the pattern, but it has not interrupted anything in the bust area. This is great for those who have fuller bust measurements but also have narrow upper chests.

Center Front Waist to Lower Vertical Bustline

This measurement is another way to refine the fit of your patterns and ensure design details, such as darts and princess seams, fall in the correct location for your body.

The lower vertical bustline falls below the apex. If you have patterns with waist darts or design details, you will want them to fall in this area. These details can create various illusions on the body. If they are too close to the center, you will look really narrow, or they will widen your appearance if placed too far toward the side seam. This happens often when sewists adjust their patterns only at the side seam. Of course, you can intentionally adjust the placement of these lines, but you do want to be aware of this area of measure.

Note: This is an optional adjustment that further divides the front waist measurement. If you have a good grasp of my method, then experiment with this adjustment. If you are still learning, then you can come back to this one after you feel comfortable with the basics.

This measurement is always adjusted at the waist between the center front and the lower vertical bustline. The bustline is not marked on your pattern, but you know right where it is. Your pattern has the apex and dart placement lines, and you know these details should fall on the vertical bustline. Therefore, you can use the base of the waist dart as your reference point when measuring.

This is also important because, as you make various garments, you want design details like collars, pleats, gathers, buttons and other items that are supposed to fall in the center front of the body to fall in the center front of the pattern. Those details should not fall to the side of the body past the apex, causing fit issues, so creating a pattern that has the correct width in these areas will further your success in sewing and fit.

Measure from the center front waist to the lower vertical bustline directly below the apex.

The Lower Vertical Bustline as a Guide

The lower vertical bustline is not a design line. It is a line of measure, but design lines and details should fall on it, such as princess seams and waist darts.

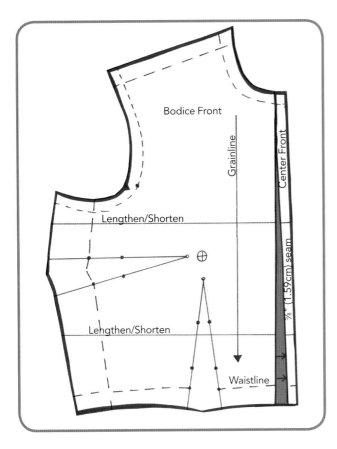

Slash-and-spread increase

Measure approximately 1" (2.5cm) from the center front at the waist of the pattern. Cut vertically up the pattern to, but not through, the neckline. Spread out the center front of the pattern at the waist by the desired amount to create the correct distance from the center to the vertical bustline (also the location of the dart). This hinge prevents disruption of the neckline.

Tips

- You can apply these adjustments to the front edge of the pattern as an alternative method, but creating a hinge by using the slash-and-spread method creates a very clear illustration of what the pattern is doing.

- A note about grain: Although you are changing the angle of the center front of the pattern, you are not affecting the grainline. Continue to use the grain as marked. If you want to cut your pattern on the fold, use the new angle (edge) of the center front of the pattern as your grainline and place it on the fold.

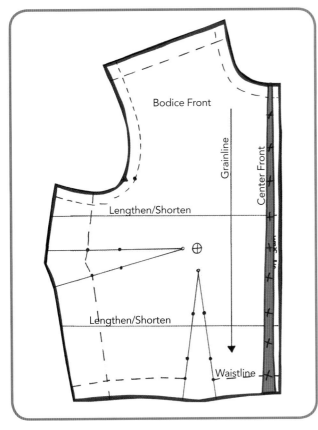

Slash-and-spread decrease

Measure approximately 1" (2.5cm) from the center front at the waist of the pattern. Cut vertically up the pattern to, but not through, the neckline to create a hinge. Shift the waist inward, deducting the amount needed to match your body measurement. The Xs indicate the portion of the pattern that is being removed.

Full Upper Back (Shoulders)

The fullest part of the back often falls over the shoulder blades, but not always. Make sure you focus on the fullest point across the back when measuring. This is key to having full range of motion when moving your arms forward and ensuring you have enough space in your garments across the back. The upper back is also a very common place to adjust a pattern for those with full upper backs or narrow shoulders.

The L-slash method, commonly associated with sleeve bicep fitting, can be useful for adjusting other pattern pieces, especially in the upper back. Many sewists have broad backs or narrow backs and shoulders, and this method works well because it changes only the area needed and leaves the rest of the pattern stationary. If you have these fitting issues, this adjustment is for you.

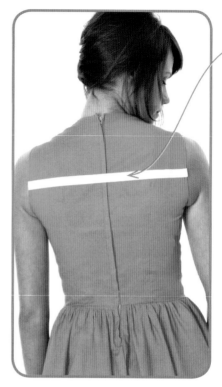

Measure across the fullest part of the back from one armhole to the other. This may or may not be the shoulder blades. *Tip:* Use garment tape to mark the correct armhole location for ease in measuring.

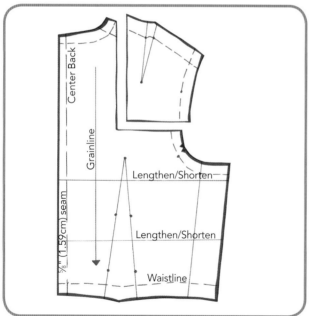

L-slash

On the upper back, you need to create a segment of the pattern that can be shifted inward or outward. If you have gone through the vertical adjustment chapter (Chapter 2), you have a back pattern that reflects the correct length for your back. Measure down from the approximate center of the shoulder to the full back area. Draw a line straight down and then draw a horizontal line through the armhole. Cut on these lines, removing the upper portion of the pattern. You now have a movable section of the pattern.

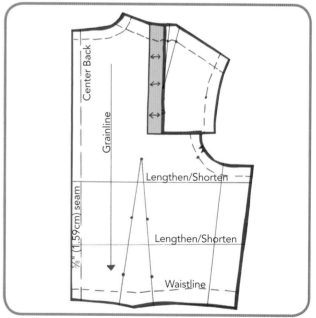

To increase

After slashing your pattern segment, shift it outward by the amount needed to increase the upper back to match your body measurement. The adjustment has changed the upper part of the pattern but not the lower part of the pattern. This is great for those with a fuller upper torso.

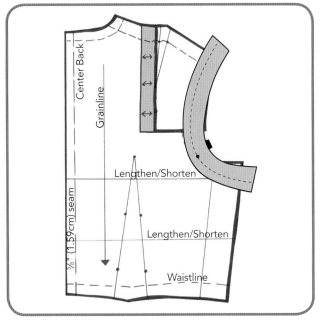

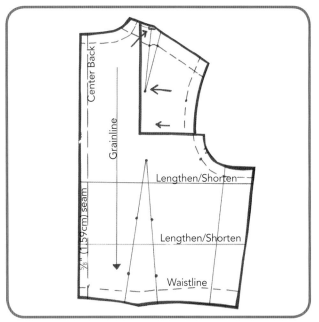

Truing the increase

True up your shoulder dart if you slashed it when creating your L-section. Notice the armhole has shifted outward to reflect your body shape. You can simply take a French curve and redraw the armhole shape or create an armhole template according to my armhole solutions in Chapter 2.

To decrease

After slashing your pattern segment, shift it inward to decrease the upper back. Notice how the adjustment has changed the upper part of the pattern but has not interrupted other areas of the pattern. You can see how the shoulder reflects a narrow back. This is great for those with fuller waists but narrow shoulders or upper backs. A slight amount of truing is required at the shoulder and armhole. Follow the armhole solutions in Chapter 2.

Tips

• *If you apply these adjustments on the back, you most likely have applied something similar to the front (usually the upper chest), so the shoulder seams should match.*

• *Don't over-fit this area. Sometimes, rather than adjusting the pattern, contouring the body is the better solution, especially for narrow shoulders. A combination of both is an option as well.*

Mid Back (Back Full Bust)

The mid-back measurement is the back half of the full-bust measurement. We have already discovered that we cannot make a generic full-bust adjustment only at the side seam. Treating the back separately from the front allows us to modify a pattern to fit its targeted areas and then mesh them together when we sew the side seams.

The mid-back section of the pattern addresses the width of the pattern across the portion of the back that falls in line with the full bust. Usually people are narrower or shorter across the back than the front. Because the counterparts for this area are the "peaks and valleys" of the breast area across the front, it stands to reason why the back would be shorter. That being said, there are exceptions to the rule, and that is why treating the front pattern separately from the back is key to the correct proportion and fit.

Measure from the side seam under the arm across the back to the other side seam. *Tip:* Use garment tape to place side seam marks vertically on the body so you start and stop at the same point of measure.

> ### Tip
>
> *If you are making a large increase or decrease across the back, you will want to combine this with other adjustments listed later in this chapter for a more evenly distributed adjustment.*

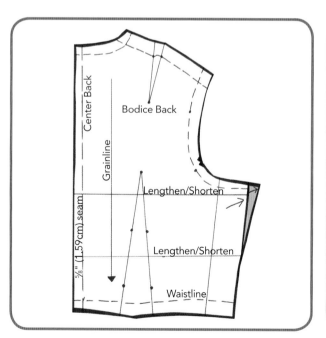

To increase
Measure your body across the back and divide that measurement in half since the pattern is half a pattern. At the top of the side seam, measure out past the side by the amount needed to add width across the back. Taper to nothing down the side seam.

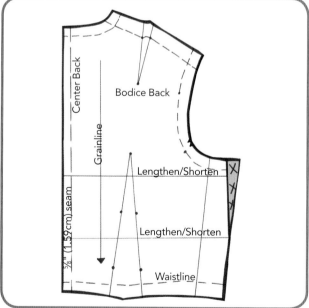

To decrease
Measure your body across the back and divide that measurement in half since the pattern is half the back. At the top of the side seam, measure inward and deduct the amount necessary to match your measurement. True up the side and transition down the side seam to create a nice taper to the natural waist. The Xs indicate the portion of the pattern that is being removed.

Back Waist

The back waist measurement is a useful measurement for dividing the full waist into more customizable sections. By treating the back separately from the front, you can address the different lengths of the waist. Most people are shorter across the back than the front; therefore, evenly adjusting a pattern on both the front waist and the back waist will not correct the fit. Have you ever had a side seam that was not straight up and down? It is possible that the pattern was too wide across the back and not wide enough across the front. This measurement will address those issues.

Width adjustments across the back waist should not be made by taking in or letting out the seam allowance or adjusting things like darts and design details, but that is often what people to do. These adjustments need to happen within the body of the pattern or on an edge of the pattern, leaving the integrity of those other details.

Measure from the side seam at the waist across the back of the body to the other side seam. *Tip:* Use garment tape to place a vertical side seam on the body. This will allow you to start and stop at the same location when you measure the front section.

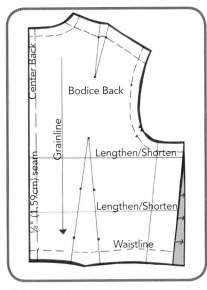

Side seam increase

This is one pattern change where you can use the side edge for the adjustment, but you are only addressing the back body measurement on the back of the pattern. Measure from the center back waist of the pattern to the side seam. Do not include darts, gathers or design details in this measurement. If you come to a dart, stop your tape measure, jump over the dart and resume measuring until you reach the side seam (do not include the seam allowance). Extend the waist outward by the amount needed. True up your side seam and taper to nothing as you straighten the side.

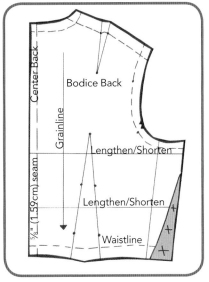

Side seam decrease

To decrease the waist at the edge of the pattern, measure from the center back waist of the pattern to the side seam. Do not include the dart or other design details. If you come to a dart, stop the tape measure, jump over the dart and resume measuring until you reach the side seam (do not include the seam allowance). Measure inward on the waist at the side seam and decrease the amount needed to match your measurement. True up your side seam. The Xs indicate the portion of the pattern that is being removed.

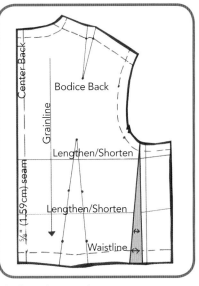

Slash-and-spread increase or decrease

The slash-and-spread method also works on the waist if you want to keep the integrity of the side seam. Not including the seam allowance, measure in approximately 1" (2.5cm) at the waist and slash up vertically on your pattern. Cut to, but not through, the edge of your pattern at the armhole. This will create a hinge. Shift the pattern open at the waist to increase, or shift the hinge inward to decrease the amount needed to match your body measurement.

Other Back Pattern Adjustments

In the preceding two sections, we addressed fitting changes at the side seam; however, on large increases or decreases, you need to distribute the change across the entire back area of the pattern. Similar to the front of a torso, pattern adjustments can be made to the center of the back pattern using the slash-and-spread method or made at the edge.

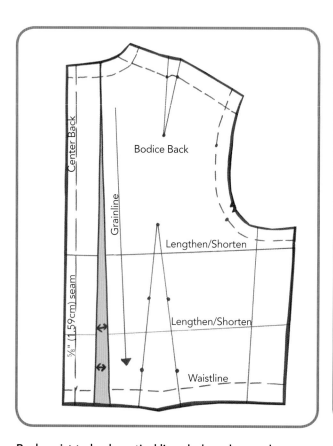

Back waist to back vertical line slash-and-spread
Back patterns often have waist darts or design lines that must fall in the correct location on the body. Similar to the front vertical bustline, you can also apply that same technique to the back. Measure at the waist over to the base of the back waist dart and compare that to your body measurement. Cut a vertical line up the back of the pattern to, but not through, the top. Shift the pattern outward to increase this distance at the waist, or shift it inward to decrease the distance from the center back to the dart. In this example, the pattern increases only at the waist. Notice that I am not adjusting the side seam. I am simply creating more room at the center back waist for correct distance.

Center back increase
If you measure your body and find that you need to add width across the back of the pattern near the center area of the back, you can simply extend the pattern evenly all the way up the pattern. This is a safe adjustment, and you can always pin out any extra during the muslin fit sample phase.

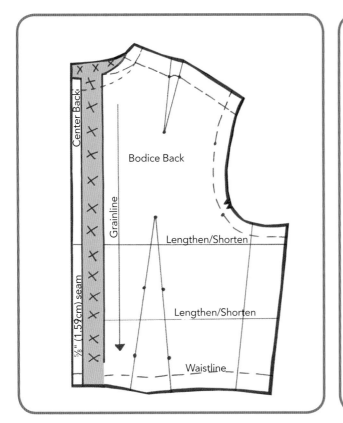

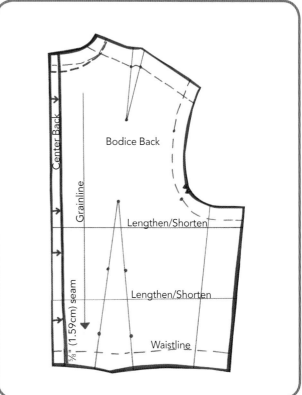

Center back decrease slash-and-spread

Measure in approximately 1" (2.5cm) at the center back waist. Draw a vertical line all the way up the pattern. Cut the center back edge apart from the pattern and shift it inward to decrease the pattern. The Xs indicate the portion of the pattern that is being removed. The back neckline will become narrower. You can clip this open during the fitting phase, or measure down on the neckline by the same amount you reduced the pattern to open it back up.

Center back decrease slash-and-spread trued

In this example, the pattern has been decreased and moved inward as noted by the red arrows. The back neckline has also been marked with a red dotted line, showing that it has been shifted downward to open it after becoming narrow from the pattern reduction.

Other Horizontal Torso Pattern Examples

As you have gone through Chapters 2 and 3 and the various ways to adjust a pattern to match your body measurements, hopefully you are starting to see that my method is very fluid. You have the freedom to apply the "measure yourself, measure your pattern" concept according to your own needs.

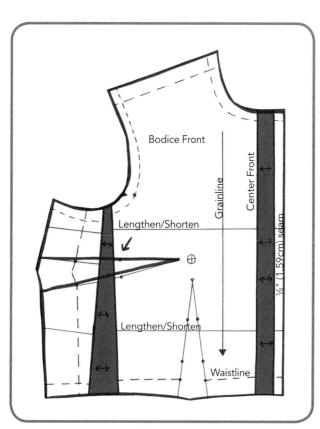

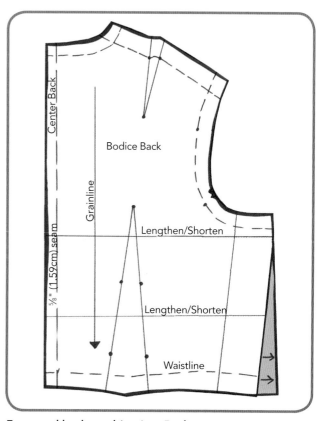

Front and back combination: Front

This pattern illustrates how a pattern might have a combination of horizontal adjustments. What do you see? The center front of the pattern has been increased with the slash-and-spread method. Notice that by doing this evenly up the entire length of the pattern, we have also increased the width at the apex to apex and the upper chest. All three areas were adjusted in one process quickly and easily. Yes, the center front neckline is temporarily longer, but this will be polished up in the fitting. The width at the waist has also been increased using the slash-and-spread method, and the dart has been trued.

Front and back combination: Back

Even though the front needed several adjustments, our back pattern only has a simple increase at the waist. Isn't it interesting to note how the increases are not distributed evenly throughout the pattern? You probably have a lightbulb going off right now, realizing that the traditional method of adjusting patterns does not truly address an individual's proper proportion and fit.

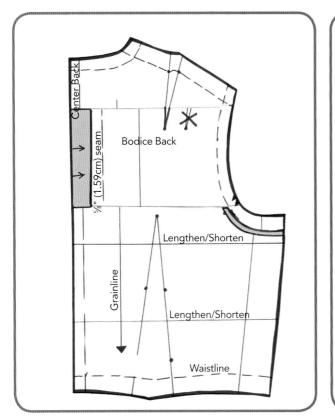

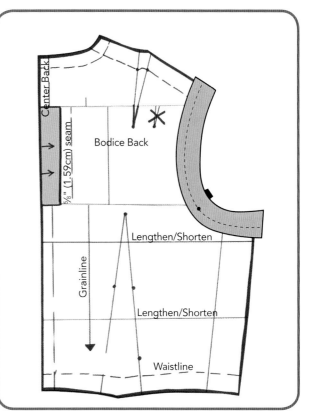

Upper full back alternate

You learned a great L-slash method for adjusting the entire upper section of the back and front pattern, but what if your pattern fits the shoulders, and you only need width below the shoulder and above the mid back? Here is how I shift fullness within a pattern. Draw two horizontal lines, one above and one below the area you need to increase. Simply shift that section outward to increase the width or shift it inward to decrease that area of the pattern. In this example, the mid-upper-back section has been shifted outward. Notice the dart tip that has been X'd out. See how far it has been shifted over? The original dart has been trued up. Armhole truing applies. See Chapter 2 for examples.

Upper full back alternate arm template

After adjusting the fullness within the upper section of the torso pattern, the armhole will have changed. It will either curve further inward or extend outward, and it will need to be trued up. Here is an example of creating an armhole template for truing the curve of the armhole. See Chapter 2 for more ideas.

Chapter 4

Vertical Lower Body Adjustments

The lower body is just as unique as the upper body when it comes to fitting. Did you know that the hiplines on the front and back of your pattern do not need to match at the side seam? Scandalous, right? They do need to be parallel to the floor, but hips can be different from the front of the pattern compared to the back, and their placement may not even line up. In this chapter, you will explore the various vertical measurements on the body that will help you create a pattern that replicates the proportion of your own unique combination of lower body shapes and curves.

Vertical Lower Body Measurement Chart

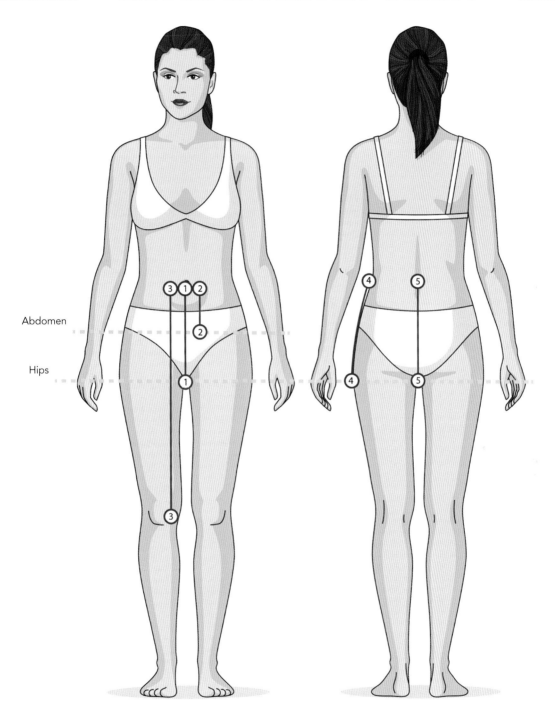

Abdomen

Hips

1	Center Front Waist to Hips	
2	Center Front Waist to Abdomen	
3	Center Front Waist to Knee	
4	Side Seam Waist to Hips	
5	Center Back Waist to Hips	

Center Front Waist to Hips

Traditionally, sewing books and patterns say that the hip area on a pattern falls approximately 7"–9" (18cm–23cm) down from the waist. Silly tradition! We all know, or you will know shortly, that there are many different lengths from the waist to one's true hip. Hiplines can be high, low or anything in between and different from the front to the back of the pattern. The most important thing is that you correct your pattern to mirror how your body looks and not according to a standard.

In this adjustment, we are addressing the front of the pattern only. Traditionally, if you adjust the front of a pattern, you do the same on the back and match the pieces at the side. For now, address only the front hip measurement. We will address the back and then join the pieces later on in the chapter.

Patterns usually have a horizontal hipline printed across the pattern. Theoretically, you could place a horizontal line anywhere on your pattern and call it the hipline. I say this because some people get really hung up on the printed lines on a pattern. It's only a reference point, and it can change, but because we have this already printed on the pattern, we can use it to adjust the pattern.

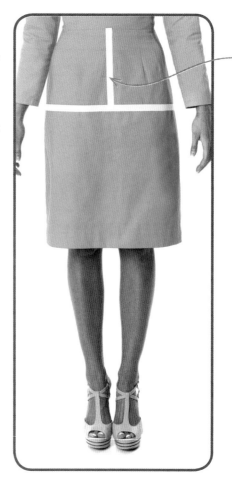

Measure down from the center of the natural waist to the fullest part of the front hips. *Tip:* Place some garment tape on the body to get a more accurate representation of the full hips.

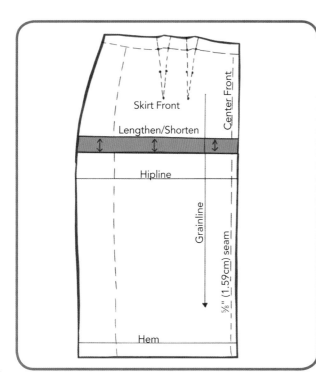

Skirt Front

Lengthen/Shorten

Center Front

Hipline

Grainline

⅝" (1.59cm) seam

Hem

Waist-to-hip increase
Measure from the center front of your pattern at the waist down to the printed hipline. Compare that vertical measurement to your own body measurement. To increase, draw a horizontal line across the pattern (below the base of the darts but above the hipline), or use the printed lengthen/shorten line and spread the pattern by the amount needed to match your body measurement.

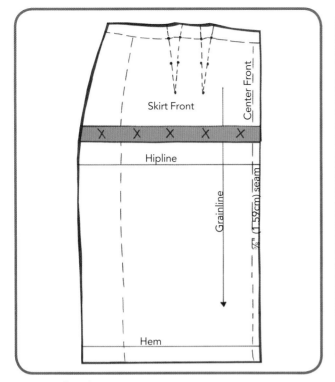

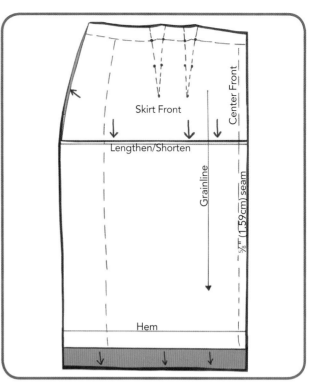

Waist-to-hip decrease

Measure from the center front of your pattern at the waist down to the printed hipline. Compare that measurement to your body measurement. If you need to decrease the pattern, cut across the printed lengthen/shorten line or create a cutting line on the pattern (below the base of the darts but above the hipline) and remove the extra amount. The Xs indicate the portion of the pattern that is being removed.

Waist-to-hip decrease trued

In this example, I have decreased the length from the waist to the hip. The red line shows where a portion of the pattern has been removed. Notice how the upper hip was trued up by taking a hip curve ruler and reshaping the hip area. I have also added back length to the bottom of the pattern. Even though the example shortens the upper portion of the pattern, I may want to keep the original length of the pattern, and adding back to the hem is the solution.

 ## Customize in the Upper Area

Lengthening or shortening a pattern is not always as simple as cutting it off at the hem. You can see in these examples that adjusting the pattern in the upper area is what customized the fit. When you lengthen, shorten or adjust in the top of the pattern, the lower edge is temporarily changed. The hem area is superficial and something to polish off in the fitting. The main area of fitting is not the bottom of your pattern.

Center Front Waist to Abdomen (optional

The abdomen can be an additional measurement to use in conjunction with the full hips or, depending on your body type and whether your abdomen is wider than your hips, it can replace the hip measurement altogether. This measurement deals with the curves of the full abdomen and is *always* an increase in the pattern. If you are fortunate enough to have a very flat midsection, then this measurement will not apply to your body. If you have a fuller upper tummy due to genetics, having children, natural changes in the body or simply too much chocolate, then this measurement will take care of contouring the pattern to the curve of your lower body.

There is no abdomen line printed on the pattern. This is one of those areas similar to my bust curve from Chapter 2 that we need to assign to a portion of the pattern. Do not overthink its placement. What do we know about the full abdomen? We know it is close to the waist, it is above the hip area of the pattern (even if it is fuller than the hips in some cases) and it affects only the front of the body. Now let's look at what our front lower body pattern is doing. We have front darts that are helping to fit the abdomen area generically for a flat tummy, and the pattern has a gradual curve down the side. These details need to correspond to our full tummy, and they show why simply using the printed lengthen/shorten line is too generic for the adjustment.

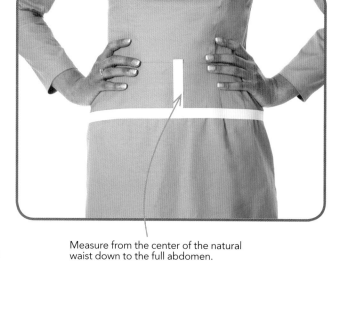

Measure from the center of the natural waist down to the full abdomen.

Hem Adjustment

Because this adjustment is an increase only, the pattern will become elongated at the hem. Simply reduce the length at the hem by the same amount that you lengthened the abdomen.

To increase

Measure 2" (5.1cm) down the center front of your pattern. Draw a horizontal line across the pattern. Measure your body from the center front of the natural waist down to your full abdomen. Your pattern needs to match this length. Cut on your horizontal line and spread your pattern by the amount needed to match your body measurement. You have now created an abdomen area on your pattern that falls within the darts and details of the pattern. True your darts.

Center Front Waist to Knee

The overall length measurements give you an idea of how long your garment and pattern need to be. They are also good checks and balances, because smaller sections of patterns should add up to these totals. The bottom portion of the pattern below the hip area and at the lower edges (hems) are solely for polishing up the length. Any other customizing should be done higher up on the pattern.

If you need to adjust your pattern solely for length, you want to do this below the hipline. Your pattern has a generic lengthen/shorten line printed above the hip, but if you use that line, the hip will drop or rise, and you do not want to adjust that area. Here we are addressing final length only and assuming everything else is correct on the pattern. Also, some length can be added at the bottom edge, but not always. Consider the shape of the lower portion of the garment and any details that may be affected if you simply use the bottom edge.

Measure from the center front waist down to the knee. You can continue this measurement down farther for longer lengths.

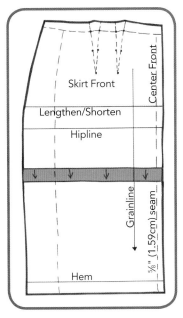

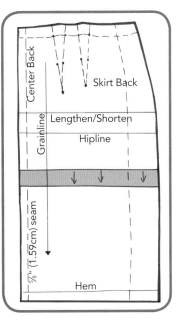

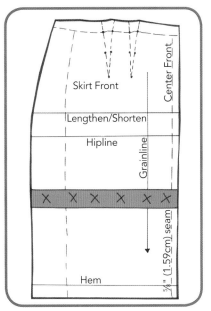

To increase length

Draw a horizontal line approximately midway between the hipline and the hem. Cut the pattern apart and add extra length to create a longer pattern. You may need to do this only on the front pattern, only on back pattern or on both depending on how you have modified the upper part of the pattern. See the end of this chapter for blending of the side seams.

To decrease length

Draw a horizontal line approximately midway between the hipline and the hem. Cut apart the pattern and deduct the amount needed to reduce the pattern to your desired length. You may need to do this only on the front pattern, only on the back pattern or on both depending on how you applied other adjustments to the pattern. The decrease amounts can also be different from the front to the back. The Xs indicate the part of the portion of the pattern that is being removed.

Side Seam Waist to Hips

The side seam to the full hip is an easy and useful measurement because some individuals' hips curve up or downward. You also might have one hip that is higher than the other. If you have one hip higher than the other, refer to the section on body contouring in Chapter 1. Uneven hips should be leveled out for a cleaner pattern adjustment and precision sewing. This is a unique measurement because it is shared by the front and the back of the body. The back hip is the same as the front hip, so any change made to the pattern is done the same on the front and back.

Measure from your natural waist at the side seam down to the hipline. Measure both sides and compare. *Tip:* Place garment tape around the fullest part of the hips to get an accurate measurement.

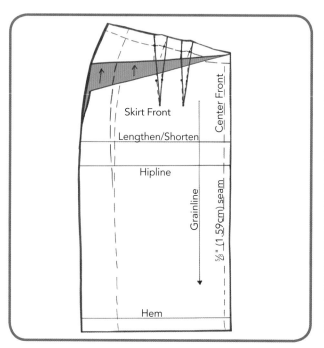

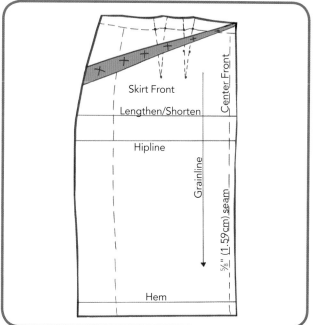

To increase
Measure down the side seam approximately halfway between the waist and the hipline. Draw a line angling up to the center front of your pattern. Cut to, but not through, the center front line. Using the hinge, spread your pattern up by the amount needed so your side seam matches your body measurement. True your darts and side seam. This will create a high hip curve.

To decrease
Measure down the side seam approximately halfway between the waist and the hipline. Draw a line angling up to the center front of your pattern. Cut to, but not through, the center front line. Using the hinge, shift the pattern down, reducing the side seam to your measurement. The Xs indicate the portion of the pattern that is being removed.

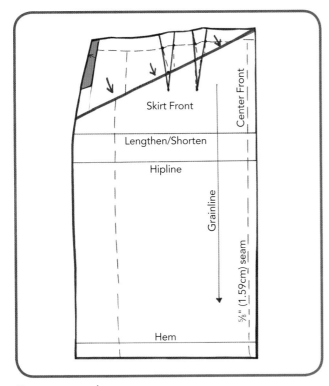

Decrease trued

True your darts and side seam after reducing the pattern. Notice how this flattens out the waist and upper side seam area. This is a very boxy shape. Can you think of anyone you know whose body reflects this shape?

Back increase

The back will be increased the same as the front increase because the front and back share this measurement. True up the back darts and side seam to match the front.

>> **Adjusting the Adjustment**

The placement line for cutting your pattern on this adjustment is fluid. I recommend approximately halfway between the waist and the hip, but you can play around with this. If you have minor hip curves, you might create a line closer to the waist. For very high curves you might start closer to the hip. Experiment.

Center Back Waist to Hips

The back hips are an interesting area to address because we see all sorts of variation. If you have been doing your Brazilian butt lift exercises (yes, I bought the workout videos—I didn't say I used them), then you have a very high hipline. Or you might have an average hipline or a very elongated back with a dropped hipline. Our backsides are an area with lots of padding. Have you ever seen someone with a "shelf" on their backside? Due to the fullness, that replaces what would be considered the natural hipline. Because of this, the back hips may not line up with the front full hips. We will delve into that more later, but the important thing is that you can measure your own body and adjust your patterns to fit your unique contours.

Remember, patterns usually have a horizontal hipline printed across the pattern. Don't get hung up on the printed lines. These are reference points that can change, but because we have this already printed on the pattern, we can use it to adjust the pattern. The adjustments will raise or lower the printed hipline to match our body proportion.

Measure from the center of the natural waist down to the fullest part of the back hips. *Tip:* Place some garment tape across the body to get a more accurate representation of the full hips.

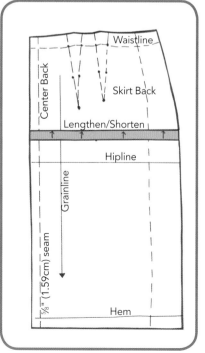

Waist-to-hip increase

Measure from the center back of your pattern at the waist down to the printed hipline. Compare that vertical measurement to your own body measurement. To increase the pattern, draw a horizontal line across the pattern (below the base of the darts but above the hipline), or use the printed lengthen/shorten line and spread the pattern by the amount needed to match your body measurement.

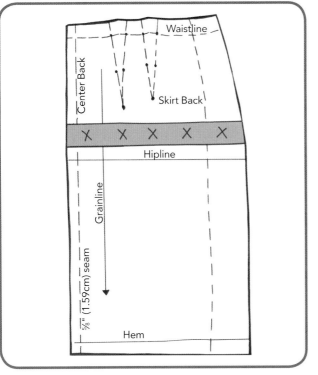

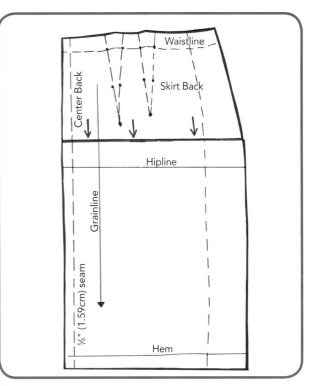

Waist-to-hip decrease

Measure from the center back of your pattern at the waist down to the printed hipline. Compare that measurement to your body measurement. If you need to decrease the pattern, cut across the printed lengthen/shorten line or create a cutting line on the pattern (below the base of the darts but above the hipline) and remove the extra amount. The Xs indicate the portion of the pattern that is being removed.

Waist-to-hip decrease trued

In this example, I have decreased the length from the waist to the hip. The red line shows where a portion of the pattern has been removed. See how the upper part of the pattern is shorter in proportion, yet the rest of the pattern has remained the same.

Tip

You might be asking yourself, how do I match my side seams if I treat the front hip separately from the back? We will cover this at the end of the chapter. This is one of those temporary changes. Remember, our adjustments are raw proportional changes.

Vertical Lower Body Combination Patterns

The combinations of vertical adjustments are unlimited due to unlimited combinations of body shapes and sizes. As you apply the vertical adjustments, you want to do most of the changes in one swift process. You should not create multiple patterns. Simply do one change and then another. After all the raw proportion adjustments are made, you can true up the pattern. Here are some examples of possible pattern scenarios for the lower body.

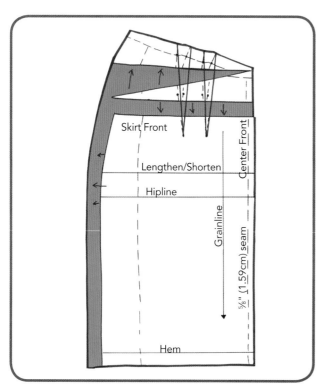

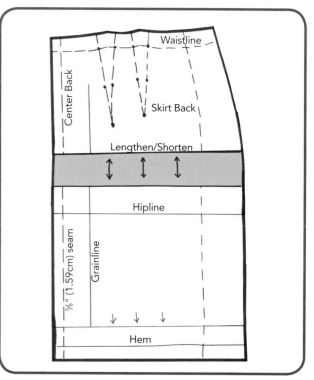

Front vertical combination

The person this pattern was created for has an abdomen adjustment in the area within the front darts. She also has a high hip. We can tell this from the angular section of the pattern that was cut and hinged. Because of that high hip, the side seam extended out, and we trued up the pattern all the way down the side seam. (If we were too generous in truing the side seam, we can trim any excess out in the fit sample stage.) Lastly, the darts were trued up and, because of the abdomen adjustment, the darts were eliminated. No adjustment was made in the hip area, so the placement matched the body measurements.

Back vertical combination

Yes, these two patterns go together. Isn't it interesting that the front had several changes, but the back looks so simple? This is just another reason why you cannot generically fit a pattern according to preprinted markings or traditional methods. On the back pattern, extra length was added, but notice the location. The length is above the hipline, which tells me this person has a lower back hipline even though it's higher in the front. These two pattern pieces now need to be joined together. I will address joining the side seams on the next page.

Tips for Blending the Lower Body Side Seams

Because we treat the front of the body separately from the back, the patterns' proportions are adjusted separately from each other. At some point, we need to join them together at the side seams, and they may not match perfectly. The solutions are pretty easy and logical, so don't get stuck on this step.

1. Pin fitting. If you have very different side seams from the front to the back, the most visual way to fit is three-dimensionally on the body. Simply pin fit the side seams together and view on the body. (***Note:*** Wear the correct undergarments. Panty lines digging into the hip will not help the fitting process. You need a natural hip curve to do this.) Unpin and adjust as necessary. Your pattern will be in the proportion and scale of your body, so you just need to smooth that side seam transition.

2. One side is shorter than the other. This is easy. Again, don't over-fit. Walk the hip curve by placing the sides next to each other to see that they blend well. If they do, then you most likely only need to add length to the shorter side. Refer to the section Center Front Waist to Knee (page 53) for basic length additions. I usually err on adding length to the shorter pattern because I can always take it out if necessary. It's much less efficient if you have to add length later.

3. Matching weird hip curves. Because we have bodies that often have lower hip curves in the back and higher abdomens in the front, and they need to be joined together, how do we address this? Some discrepancies are minor, and if that is the case, I simply pin them together in the muslin fitting. Some differences are major and take a little more care or a combination of fitting skills. The body may not always have a smooth hip curve.

First, I consider body contouring. It is possible that I need to pad the side seam with some light layers of interlining or batting to fill in the cracks and make a natural shape to fit to. It might be as simple as wearing a different foundation garment, or I may need to visually pin the seam together while on the body. Some things cannot be entirely addressed on paper and need to be fitted on the body. By combining techniques, we can easily address any area of fit without anxiety.

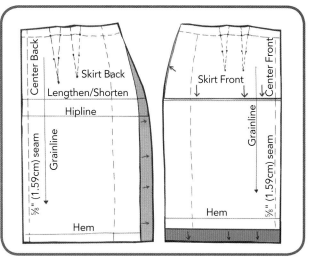

We treat the front separately from the back during adjustments. However, we do need to blend the front side seam to the back side seam either on the pattern or during the fitting.

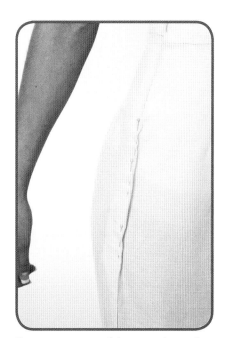

If you are not sure of the exact shape of the hip curve when adjusting your pattern, or if the curves are different from the front to back, you can blend the seams on your fit pattern. Baste or pin the side seam and then pin fit it to the contour of your body on the muslin sample.

Horizontal Lower Body Adjustments

If you have hips that measure 40" (102cm) and a pattern that measures 36" (91cm) at the hips, where do you add the extra 4" (10.2cm) of fullness needed to go around the body? Often students will say to divide the amount by the four side seams, making equal additions of 1" (2.5cm). Other sewists let out the darts and seam allowances to account for the extra width of the pattern. The darts are there to contour the pattern to your body, and you need the seam allowances. Evenly distributing the fullness among the side seams does work to make the garment go around the body, but are you increasing in the right location? You might need all 4" (10.2cm) across the back or 3" (7.6cm) in the back and only 1" (2.5cm) on the front pattern.

There are so many figure variations that generic pattern markings and traditional total adjustments simply do not make a pattern that reflects your true body shape and contours. At this point, you should have a pattern that is correct vertically. In this chapter, we will take a look at distributing fullness around the lower body again, treating the front separately from the back.

This chapter assumes you have completed the vertical lower body adjustments, and we will now focus on perfecting the width.

Horizontal Lower Body Measurement Chart

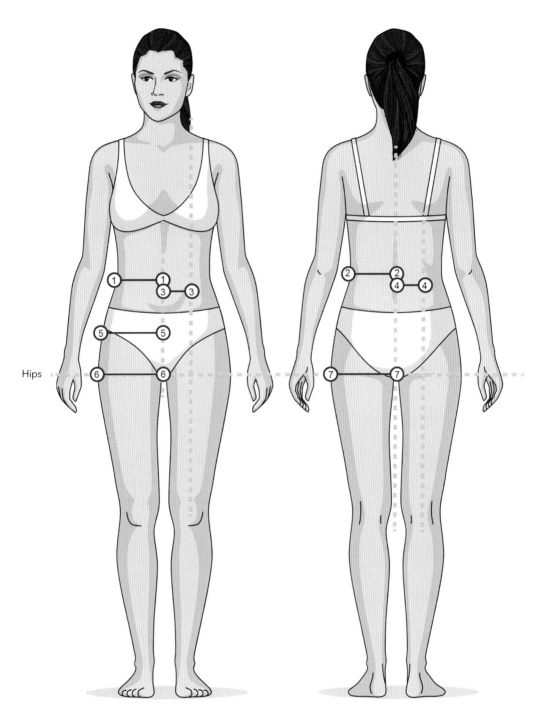

1	CF Waist to Side Seam		
2	CB Waist to Side Seam		
3	CF Waist to Lower Vertical Bustline		
4	CB Waist to Back Vertical Line		

5	CF to Side Seam at Abdomen		
6	CF to Side Seam at Hips		
7	CB to Side Seam at Hips		

CF = Center Front
CB = Center Back

Center Front Waist to Side Seam

Many sewists associate the waist measurement with the torso and often ask me why I take waist measurements on the lower body. However, if you are making a skirt or lower body garment, you need to have a stopping point, and the waist is it. Even if you are making a dress or one-piece garment, the intersection of the waist with the lower body has to be addressed on both the torso and lower body sections of the pattern. If you make certain torso adjustments horizontally, those same adjustments will now be applied to the lower body pattern.

Remember as you use the waist measurement, you are measuring the natural waistline, not a design line such as a dropped waist that we often see in ready-to-wear garments. If you like these dropped or raised waists, you can add them after pattern fitting as a design detail.

Width adjustments like the front waist should not be made by taking in or letting out the seam allowance, darts or other design details, but that is often what people do. These adjustments need to happen within the body of the pattern or on an edge of the pattern.

Measure from the center front of the natural waist line to the side seam. This is half your body measurement across the front.

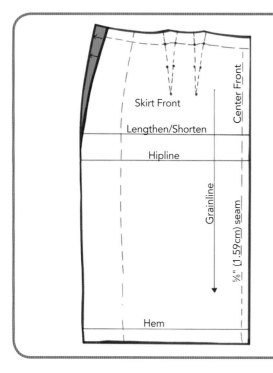

Side seam increase

This is one pattern change where you can use the side edge for the adjustment, but you are only addressing the front body measurement on the front of the pattern. Measure from the center front of the pattern to the side seam. Do not include darts or design details in this measurement. If you come to a dart, stop your tape measure, jump over the dart and resume measuring until you reach the side seam (do not include the seam allowance). Extend the waist outward the amount needed. True up your side seam and taper to nothing as you straighten the side.

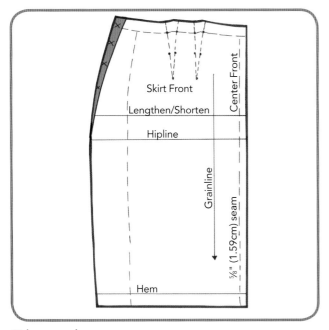

Side seam decrease

You can decrease the waist by also using the edge of the pattern. Measure from the center front of the pattern to the side seam. Do not include the dart or other design details. If you come to a dart, stop the tape measure, jump over the dart and resume measuring until you reach the side seam (do not include the seam allowance). Measure inward on the waist and decrease the amount needed to match your measurement. True up your side seam. The Xs indicate the portion of the pattern that is being removed.

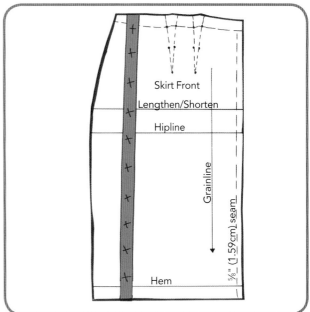

Slash-and-spread increase or decrease

The slash-and-spread method also works on waist adjustments if you want to keep the integrity of the side seam. Not including the seam allowance, measure in approximately 1" (2.5cm) at the waist and slash down vertically on your pattern. You cannot create a hinge on the lower body pattern, so as you shift the pattern outward to increase or inward to decrease, it will need to be even all the way down to the hem (unless a silhouette style would allow for the hinge). In our pattern here, the Xs represent a decrease in the pattern (indicating the portion being removed).

Note: As you make this adjustment, it also decreases or increases the hip area and the width of the pattern all the way to the hem. This is a great uniform way to address all width-fitting areas at once. It also works well if you have no major shape issues at the side seam.

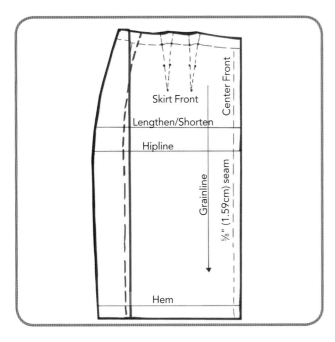

Slash-and-spread trued

In this pattern, I have decreased the pattern and removed the excess width. The red line indicates where the adjustment took place, and the red dotted lines are the trued-up stitching lines and seam allowance. Although I reduced the pattern width within the body of the pattern, the generous seam allowance is left intact.

Center Back Waist to Side Seam

The area of the body where the waist intersects the lower body on the back is a common area for fitting issues. Usually you see pooling fabric (which is a length issue and has an easy fix in the fitting phase), or the back is too long and the side seams angle toward the front rather than hanging straight up and down. Sewists often fix this by simply taking in the center back seam, creating fit and proportion issues. These things happen because the back waist measurement is often shorter across than the front, but the sewist or the pattern makes it wider than necessary. So, next time you take a total waist circumference, keep in mind it does not divide out evenly between the front and the back.

Measure from the center back waist to the side seam. This will be half your back waist measurement.

Slash, Spread, Repeat

The slash-and-spread method used on the front of the pattern is also an option for the back of the pattern. See the preceding section to review these instructions.

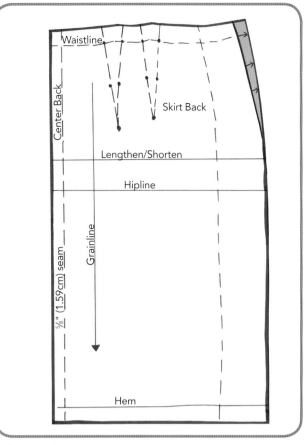

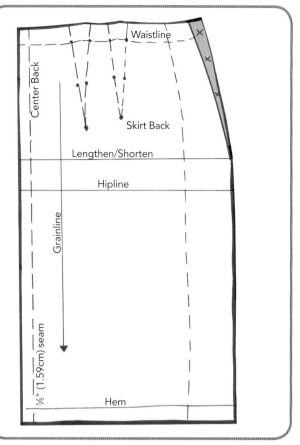

Side seam increase

This is one pattern change where you can use the side edge for the adjustment, but you are only addressing the back body measurement on the back of the pattern. Measure from the center back of the pattern to the side seam. Do not include darts or things like gathers and design details in this measurement. If you come to a dart, stop your tape measure, jump over the dart and resume measuring until you reach the side seam (do not include the seam allowance). Extend the waist outward the amount needed. True up your side seam and taper to nothing as you straighten the side.

Side seam decrease

To decrease the waist at the edge of the pattern, measure from the center back of the pattern to the side seam. Do not include the dart or other design details. If you come to a dart, stop the tape measure, jump over the dart and resume measuring until you reach the side seam (do not include the seam allowance). Measure inward on the waist at the side seam and decrease the amount needed to match your measurement. True up your side seam. The Xs indicate the portion of the pattern that is being removed.

>> Splitting Up an Adjustment

If you find you are making very large increases or decreases at the side, you might need to divide that amount between the side seam and the center back of the pattern. How will you know if that is necessary? Follow the next two measurements referencing the vertical line and you will know if your pattern needs to be changed in the center back.

Center Front Waist to Lower Vertical Bustline

The lower vertical bustline was used in the vertical torso adjustments, and we know it should fall directly below the apex. If you have a dart or design detail that falls on the lower vertical bustline, you want the lower body details to fall on the same line and match up. This is an important measurement because having the correct width across the center front of your garment will prevent pleats from buckling, darts from pulling or looking too narrow, and gathers from hanging straight. These details should not fall to the side of the body because fit issues and unflattering lines can occur.

This measurement is always adjusted at the waist between the center front and the lower vertical bustline. The bustline is not marked on your pattern, but we know how to locate it. According to our torso lessons from Chapter 2, our pattern has apex and dart placement lines, and we know these details should fall on the vertical bustline. Therefore, we can use the base of the waist dart as our reference point when measuring.

Measure from the center front waist to the bottom of the lower vertical bustline.

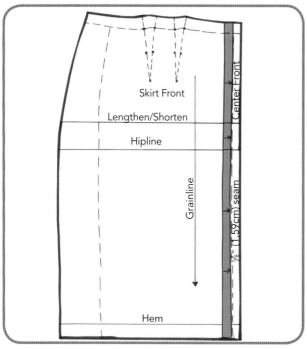

Slash-and-spread increase

Measure over approximately 1" (2.5cm) from the center front waist of the pattern. Draw and cut a vertical line down the pattern. Spread the center front of the pattern at the waist the desired amount to create the correct distance from the center to the lower vertical bustline (also the location of the dart). You will not be able to create a hinge, and the increase will be an even amount down the center. *Note:* You have also increased the hip area of the pattern. This is a clean adjustment and great for creating the correct proportion at the center of your pattern.

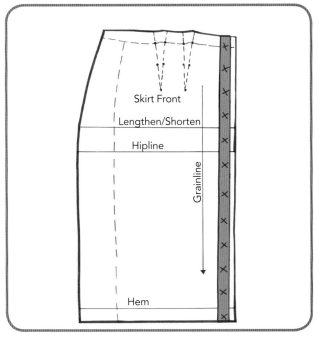

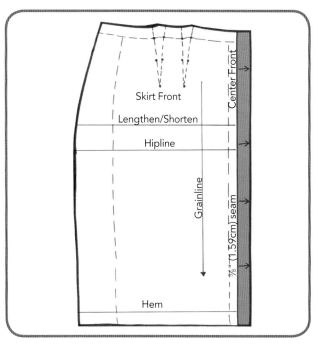

Slash-and-spread decrease

Measure over approximately 1" (2.5cm) from the center front waist of the pattern. Draw and cut a vertical line down the pattern. Shift the waist inward, deducting the amount needed to match your body measurement. The Xs indicate the portion of the pattern that is being removed. *Note:* You have also reduced the hip area of the pattern by the same amount.

Center front edge increase

Because the edge of this pattern is straight up and down, you may choose to simply extend the center front edge of the pattern the amount needed to match your body measurement. Make sure you use a ruler and increase the pattern equally all the way down. The extended edge will be your new center front line.

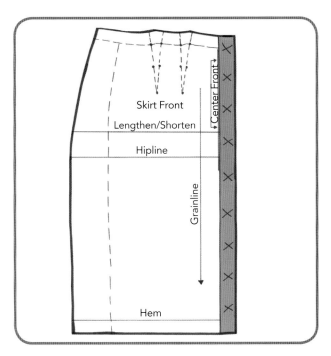

Center front edge decrease

The same process applies as increasing the center front edge of the pattern. Because the edge of the pattern is straight up and down, you may choose to simply measure inward and reduce the pattern right on the edge. Deduct the same amount all the way down the pattern so you have a nice, straight center front. The Xs indicate the portion of the pattern that is being removed.

 Watch the Numbers

As you are increasing or decreasing this area of the pattern, remember you are using half the body measurement because your pattern is half the front of the body.

Center Back Waist to Back Vertical Line

Back patterns often have fitting details such as waist darts and design lines that should fall in the correct location on the body. Similar to the front vertical line placement, we can use the same technique to ensure the correct fit and placement of the back. Your back vertical line could be toward the center or closer to the side seam. This is a very fluid area because it is not marked. The most important rule is to place the line where it looks the best on your body contours.

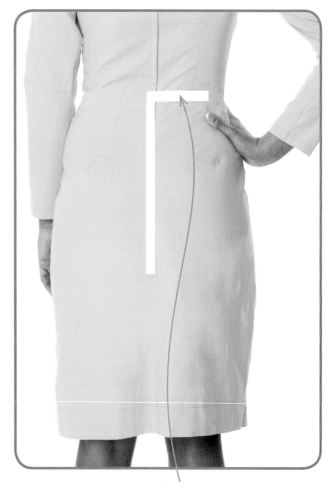

Measure from the center back waist to the correct location for the back waist dart. This is often midway between the center back and the side seam, but the placement can vary. *Tip:* Use garment tape to place a line on the torso and visualize where the correct location is on your body.

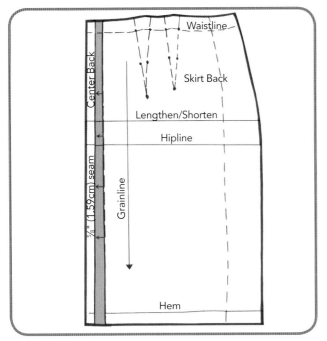

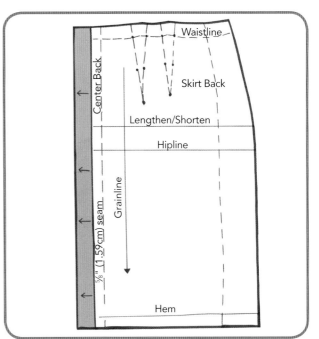

Slash-and-spread increase or decrease

Measure from the center back waist over to the base of the back waist dart and compare that to your body measurement. Cut a vertical line down the back of the pattern. Shift the pattern outward to increase this distance at the waist, or shift it inward to decrease the distance from the center back to the dart. In this example, the pattern increases only at the waist. Notice we are not adjusting the side seam. We are simply creating more (or less) room at the center back waist for correct distance. This adjustment will add or remove width all the way down the pattern, increasing or decreasing the hip and hem area.

Center back increase

Because the center back of the pattern is straight up and down, you can easily create a seamless increase all the way down the center back. Measure over the amount needed to match your body and make a clean addition all the way down. This adjustment will add width evenly all the way down the hip and hem area.

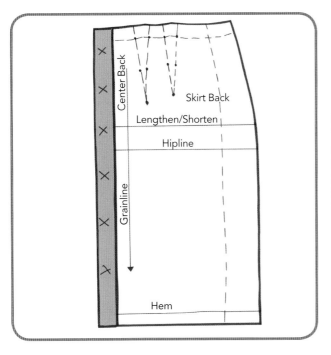

Center back decrease

You can easily decrease the center back in the same fashion as increasing it. The center back is straight up and down, so you simply measure inward the amount needed to reduce your pattern. Remove the same amount all the way down the pattern. Remember, this will also reduce your hip and hem area. The Xs indicate the portion of the pattern that is being removed.

Center Front to Side Seam at Abdomen (optional)

If you are using the abdomen measurement, you have a full tummy area across the front of your body above the hipline. The abdomen is *always* an increase in the pattern. Sometimes the abdomen measures larger or longer than the hips, and in that case, the abdomen replaces the need to do a full hip adjustment in the front. This is because the abdomen is fuller and the garment will be hanging from the fullest point. So you may not use this measurement at all (if you are lucky enough to have a flat tummy). You may adjust this width measurement in conjunction with the hip, or you may use it in place of the full front hip measurement.

There is no abdomen line printed on the pattern. If you have a full abdomen, make sure you have done the vertical placement of the abdomen line according to the lesson in Chapter 4. This adjustment assumes you have found and corrected the pattern for your abdomen line.

Measure from the center front abdomen to the side seam.

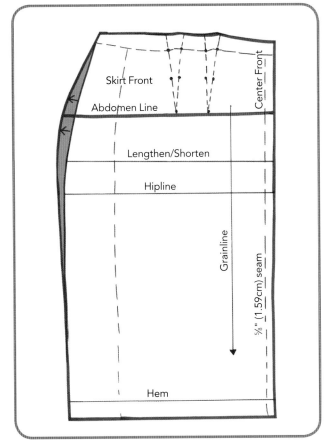

Side seam increase

On your abdomen line, measure from the center of the pattern to the side seam. This is half of the front pattern. Compare this distance to half of your front abdomen measurement. To increase the abdomen, extend the side seam for more width. True up your side seam, taper to nothing at the waist (because you may not need to add at the waist) and transition down the side seam to nothing. This adds width only across the abdomen area on the pattern. **Note:** You will never increase the abdomen at the center of the pattern.

Slash-and-spread increase

If you want to keep the integrity of the side seam, you can increase the pattern using the slash-and-spread method. Measure in approximately 2" (5.1cm) from the side seam. Draw and cut a vertical line down the pattern. Spread the pattern open the amount needed so the abdomen is now the correct width. Notice how this method also increases the waist and hip areas. There is no way to prevent this because creating a hinge will not work on this adjustment. This works well if you want to do all the adjustments at once.

 Removing or Deducting Added Width

If you like the slash-and-spread process but do not need excess at the waist, you can deduct some of the added amount at the waist on the side seam.

Center Front to Side Seam at Hips

The width at the full hip is a key area affecting how garments on the lower body drape and hang. If the garment is too tight in this area, it will create pull lines and skew the bottom of your clothing. We have not addressed ease in any other measurement lessons. In this lesson, we will adjust the pattern directly from our measurements to the pattern by adding a small amount of ease. In the full hip area of the body, there is a starting standard for movement ease (for actions such as walking and sitting), or what I call "wiggle room," and you may include it if you like. Add an additional 1" (2.5cm) to your front hip measurement and proceed with the adjustments. More information on ease will be discussed in Chapter 8.

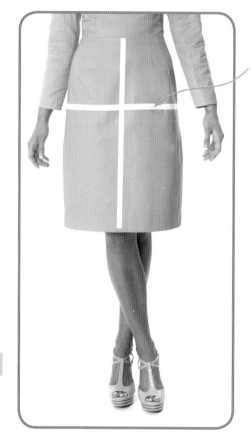

Measure from the center front of the full hip to the side seam.

Using the Fullest Part of the Body

If your abdomen is fuller across the front than your hips, the abdomen will replace the full hip because the garment needs to hang off the fullest part of the lower body. If that is the case, omit this adjustment and refer to the abdomen process in the preceding lesson.

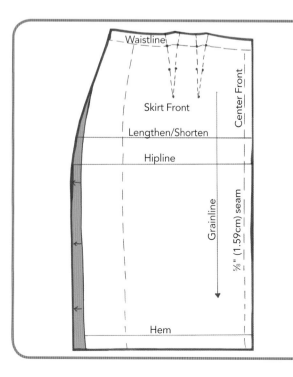

Side seam increase

Measure from the center of the pattern to the side at the full hipline. This is half of the front pattern. Compare this distance to half of your front full hip measurement. At the edge of the pattern at the hipline, extend the pattern outward the amount needed to match your measurement. You will add this same amount all the way down the pattern to the hem. Because you are only addressing the hip measurement, you will transition and taper the edge of the pattern above the hipline, thus not increasing the waist.

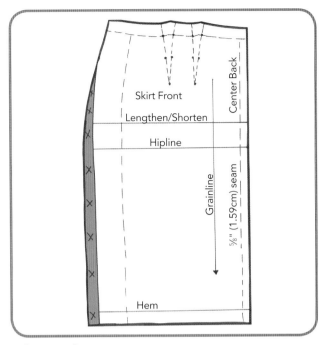

Side seam decrease

At the full hip on the pattern, you will make a reduction, decreasing the full front hip. Compare your body measurement to your pattern measurement. At the edge of the pattern on the hipline, measure inward the amount needed to decrease the hip. Continue to remove the same amount down the pattern to the hem. You are not changing the waist, so taper the pattern above the full hipline to the original waist. The Xs indicate the portion of the pattern that is being removed. Notice how the side of the pattern has a flatter hipline. Have you ever seen anyone with baggy fitting hips? In alterations, we call this "removing the saddlebags."

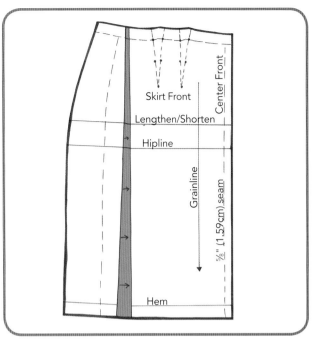

Slash-and-spread increase

If you want to keep the integrity of the side seam, you can increase the pattern using the slash-and-spread method. Measure in approximately 2" (5.1cm) from the side seam. Draw and cut a vertical line up the pattern from the hem to the waist. Cut to, but not through, the waist. Spread the pattern open the amount needed so the hip is now the correct width. Because the hip is farther down on the pattern, you can create a hinge to open up the pattern. By doing this, the hem will become wider, creating more of an A-line effect, but it works well if you do not need to increase the waist.

 Tip

If your pattern is half of a body section, like the half skirt front illustrated here, remember to use half of your body measurement.

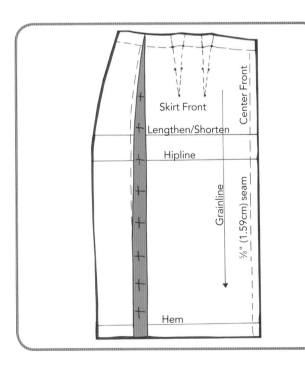

Slash-and-spread decrease

Measure in approximately 2" (5.1cm) from the side seam. Draw and cut a vertical line on the pattern from the hem to the waist. Cut to, but not through, the waist. Decrease the pattern by shifting the outer edge toward the center, deducting a portion of the pattern needed to make the hips match your body measurement. The Xs indicate the portion of the pattern that is being removed. *Note:* There is a limit to the amount you can reduce the pattern using the slash-and-spread method because the hem will become narrower than the hips. In this case, you can extend the lower edge of the pattern at the hem or use the side seam adjustment.

Center Back to Side Seam at Hips

Just like on the front of the body, the width at the back full hip is a key area affecting how garments on the lower body drape and hang. If the garment is too tight in this area, it will create pull lines and skew the bottom of your clothing. An interesting note about the back full hipline is that it can be higher, lower or simply at a different location compared to the front of the body. This is why it is so critical to treat the back pattern separately. You will have some polishing to do at the side seams when you bring the front and back together, but that is all tweaking. The most important thing is to get your back pattern to mirror the shape of your body.

A note on ease: So far we have only addressed additional ease in our previous front hip adjustment. It applies here as well with the back. In Chapter 8, I provide more tips on working with ease; however, in the full hip area of the body, there is a starting standard for movement ease ("wiggle room"). You may include it if you like at this point. Add an additional 1" (2.5cm) to your back hip measurement and proceed with the adjustments. If you feel you have a very large back hip, you might increase this to an additional 2" (5.1cm) to your total back hip measurement.

Measure from the center back of the full hip to the side seam.

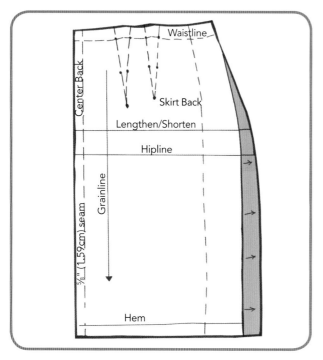

Side seam increase

Measure from the center of the pattern to the side at the full hipline. This is half of the back pattern. Compare this distance to half of your back full hip measurement. At the hipline on the edge of the pattern, extend outward by the amount needed to match your measurement. You will add this same amount all the way down the pattern to the hem. Because you are only addressing the hip measurement, you will transition and taper the edge of the pattern above the hipline, thus not increasing the waist.

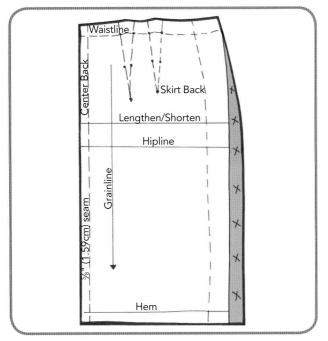

Side seam decrease

At the full hip on the pattern, you will make a reduction, decreasing the full back hip. Compare your body measurement to your pattern measurement. At the edge of the pattern on the hipline, measure inward by the amount needed to decrease the hip. Continue with the same amount down the pattern to the hem. You are not changing the waist, so taper the pattern above the full hipline to the original waist. The Xs indicate the portion of the pattern that is being removed. Notice how the side of the pattern has a flatter hipline. The decrease has an entirely different shape than the hip with a full curve.

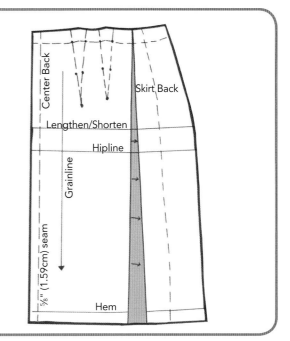

Slash-and-spread increase

If you want to keep the integrity of the side seam, you can increase the pattern using the slash-and-spread method. Measure approximately 2" (5.1cm) in from the side seam. Draw and cut a vertical line up the pattern from the hem to the waist. Cut to, but not through, the waist. Spread the pattern open by the amount needed so the hip is now the correct width. Because the hip is farther down on the pattern, you can create a hinge to open up the pattern. By doing this, the hem will become wider, creating more of an A-line effect, but it works well if you do not need to increase the waist.

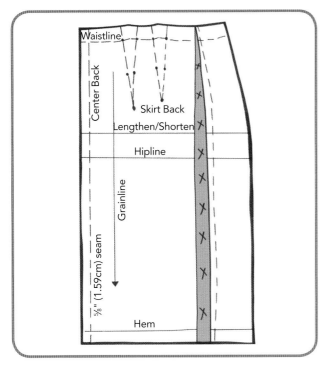

Slash-and-spread decrease

Measure approximately 2" (5.1cm) in from the side seam. Draw and cut a vertical line on the pattern from the hem to the waist. Cut to, but not through, the waist. Decrease the pattern by shifting the outer edge toward the center, deducting the portion of the pattern needed to make the hips match your body measurement. The Xs indicate the portion of the pattern that is being removed. *Note:* There is a limit to the amount you can reduce the pattern using the slash-and-spread method, because the hem will become narrower than the hips. In this case, you can extend the lower edge of the pattern at the hem or use the side seam adjustment.

Horizontal Lower Body Combinations

In this chapter, we have treated each body measurement as a separate adjustment on the pattern. As you become better at taking body measurements and comparing them to your pattern to figure out which areas to target and modify, you will see that you can tackle several measurements at once, making this an even more efficient way to address fit issues easily and quickly before you sew a single stitch. The combinations are unlimited, but here are a few to get you thinking.

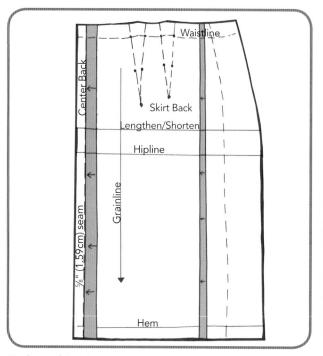

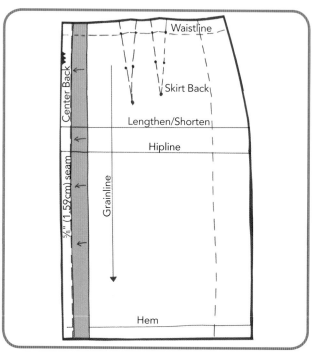

Back combination

What areas of the pattern have been adjusted in this example? We see two vertical lines that have been spread apart, and that looks pretty simple, but there is more going on here with the fit of the pattern. The center back has been lengthened from the center to the back vertical line, increasing the distance from the waist to the dart. This adjustment also adds to the waist measurement. It also continues right down the pattern to the hem, so we have increased the hip and hem as well. That is four adjustments in one slash of the pattern. Notice the additional increase toward the side seam. We could not add everything at the center back because that area would be too wide. The additional increase was added here, and it continues down, increasing the hem and hip an additional amount. Wow! All that in two simple slash-and-spread lines. You could apply the same process to the front of a pattern. Maybe that piece would include some decreasing of the pattern. You can see what body measurements do to fit and how treating a full waist or full hip measurement as one will not address those important custom changes.

Back single adjustment

Some pattern adjustments are quick and efficient. There is only one vertical slash-and-spread line on this example, and it evenly increases the waist, hip and center back waist to the dart placement. In only a few minutes, you can compare your body measurements to your pattern, do a quick adjustment and save tons of time. There's no need to cut apart a fitting sample because it does not go around your body, only to then sew a new sample. Or, worse yet, having to discard a garment in the fashion fabric all because of a simple error in measurement application.

Applying the Method to Pants

The process of adjusting a pattern for pants is the same as demonstrated throughout these lessons and with any garment. You will measure sections of the body and then measure that same area on the pattern. Some vertical areas of measure will match pretty literally to the body so details of the pants will fall on the body correctly, while some horizontal areas will measure larger due to necessary movement ease (especially bending) and possibly more design and silhouette ease to create different styles (think palazzo pants). With pants, fabric characteristics will be even more important in the application of ease and fit on top of the body measurements. Always finalize fit with a muslin fit sample.

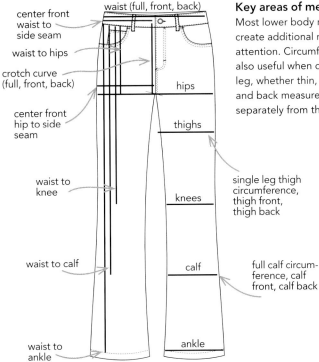

center front waist to side seam

waist to hips

crotch curve (full, front, back)

center front hip to side seam

waist to knee

waist to calf

waist to ankle

waist (full, front, back)

hips

thighs

single leg thigh circumference, thigh front, thigh back

knees

calf

full calf circumference, calf front, calf back

ankle

Key areas of measure for pants

Most lower body measurements apply to pants, and you can create additional measurements for areas that need special attention. Circumference measurements of individual legs are also useful when contouring a pattern to the curvature of the leg, whether thin, muscular or full. This includes separate front and back measurements. Remember to adjust the front pattern separately from the back.

> **Tip**
>
> *For "low rise" styles, always adjust your pattern and sewn fit sample to your natural waist so you have a consistent placement of fit. After the final fitting, draw in that style line and create the shorter cut. In reality, low rise is not really fitting the rise; it is more like shortening the upper portion of the pants below the natural waistline.*

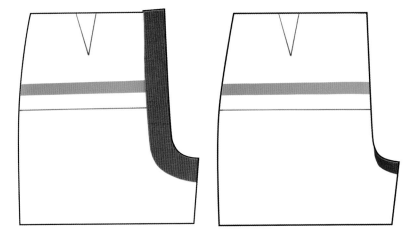

Crotch curve template

Similar to the armhole template in Chapter 2, a crotch curve template is useful in pants fitting. Trace the edge of your unaltered pattern. Next, adjust your pattern for the waist to hip measurement. If a change unnecessarily makes it longer or shorter, you can place the template at the center front waist and trace back the original shape. The fit change is in the pattern, but not in the crotch area. Place the template behind the pattern, and the pink area indicates the area that has been added back.

Chapter 6

Vertical Arm Adjustments

Sleeves have a reputation for being difficult to fit. Sewists often hyper-fit and create sleeve patterns that reflect their arms exactly, then try to join an oddly shaped sleeve to an oddly shaped armhole, which can be a difficult task for even the most experienced seamstress.

In reality, the perfect fit for sleeves happens in the pattern and is surprisingly very easy and quick to achieve. By addressing a few length and width measurements, you can create a sleeve pattern that reflects your arm exactly in proportion. After that, fit is simply a matter of pin fitting the cap during your fitting session and, voilà! The perfect sleeve!

You might be holding your breath and expecting all sorts of issues with your sleeve, but forget about all the drama and discussion traditionally linked to sleeve fitting. From now on, you only need to apply a few measurements. You can cross this off your bucket list of things to master in sewing because you will truly enjoy making sleeves with ease. Let's look at vertical arm measurements and pattern adjustments.

Vertical Arm Measurement Chart

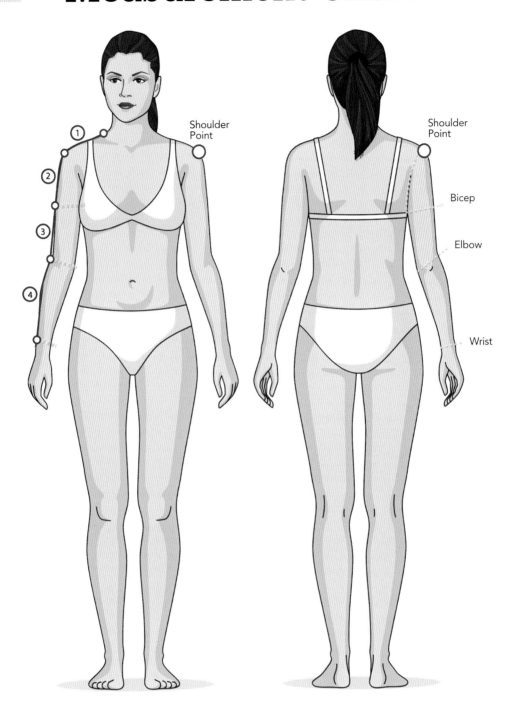

Shoulder Point

Shoulder Point

Bicep

Elbow

Wrist

1 Shoulder Length (Neck to Shoulder)

2 Cap Height (Shoulder to Bicep)

3 Bicep to Elbow

4 Elbow to Wrist

Shoulder Length: Neck to Shoulder Point

The shoulder point is a protruding bone on the arm where the arm joins the body at the shoulder. To find it, hold your arm straight out to the side and lift upward. You should be able to feel a slight indentation where this joint is located. Some people have forward-tilting shoulder points, while other people have shoulders that have a sharp angle toward the neck, shoulders that angle forward, shoulders that angle toward the back or just average-shaped shoulders. This is an area where you can easily create an artificial shoulder seam prior to measuring and correct fit issues with some basic contouring tricks (a much better option than trying to sew an odd shape). See Chapter 8 on fitting for these easy solutions.

Measure where the shoulder seam is located on the body from the neck toward the shoulder point.

Cap Height: Shoulder Point to Full Bicep

Fitting instructions often state to never adjust the cap of the sleeve, but in reality it is an easy area of the pattern to correct and is often the missing detail for obtaining a perfect-fitting sleeve. The cap of the sleeve is not simply the outer edge of the upper sleeve. It is the entire area from the shoulder point to the bicep. This length on the pattern may or may not match the proportion of your body. If you have a shorter cap height, simply removing length from the edge will not scale the pattern to your arm and correct the fit issues. You need to correct the length within the area of measure. If you have a longer cap height, you also need to adjust within the area of measure and not just at the edge—a common mistake that sewists make.

Measure from the shoulder point down to the fullest part of the arm or bicep. *Tip:* Place garment tape around the arm to find the full bicep. The bicep is often in line with the full bust, but it can sit above or below depending on your body shape.

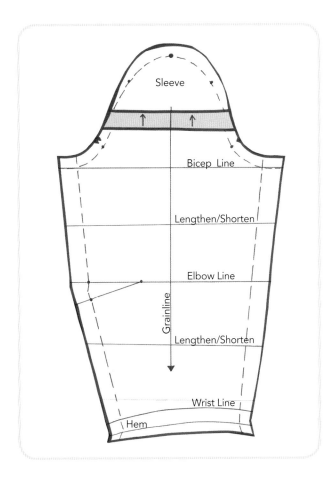

Cap increase

Approximately halfway between the shoulder point and the bicep, draw a horizontal line across the cap of the sleeve. Cut and spread the pattern by the amount necessary to increase and match your own measurement. Use a French curve or flexible ruler and true the edge of the pattern on the front and back of the sleeve where it was increased.

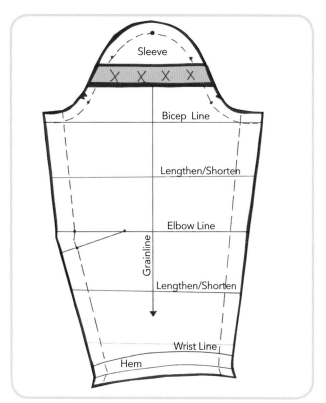

Cap decrease

Approximately halfway between the shoulder point and the bicep, draw a horizontal line across the cap of the sleeve. Cut on this line. To decrease, overlap the upper part of the cap over the lower part of the cap. Cut away the amount necessary to decrease the cap height. The Xs indicate the portion of the pattern that is being removed. True the outer edge of the cap by using a French curve or flexible ruler.

Cap decrease polished sleeve

In this example, the sleeve cap has been shortened according to the process at left. The sleeve has a very obvious shorter cap height. This is a great example because it illustrates that just because a pattern provides you with a certain sleeve shape, that does not mean it will always fit. This is a pattern for a real person with a very short cap height. **Note:** The same adjustments were not necessary on the torso of the pattern. Remember to treat each pattern piece separately, especially when it comes to sleeves.

 ## A Note on Sleeve Cap Ease

The sleeve cap is not an area that needs a lot of extra ease vertically, so the pattern will match your measurements pretty literally. You can add an extra ½" (1.3cm) to your length measurement if you want a little extra wiggle room. Adding too much more will lengthen your sleeve and may not match your arm. In Chapter 8, I will discuss adding extra ease if you happen to be padding out shoulders, lengthening armholes and using a few more tricks for arms and sleeves.

Bicep to Elbow

This midsection of the arm is a common area that needs adjustment to create a sleeve pattern that replicates the shape of the arm. Because it falls below the cap and above the lower part of the arm, it needs to be treated separately, especially for those who have extra arm fullness. Most patterns will have a printed lengthen/shorten line near the wrist, but that does not add length to the midsection and address this area.

With any pattern adjustments, you want to increase or decrease within the area of measure and not on the edge unless noted. The same applies to the midsection of the arm.

Focus on Key Areas

Arms have an unlimited combination of lengths in the three key vertical areas of the pattern. You can see how easy it is to make a sleeve that will fit you exactly.

Measure from the full bicep down to the elbow.

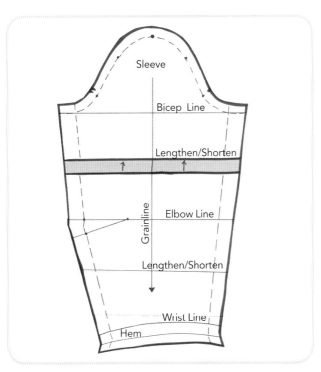

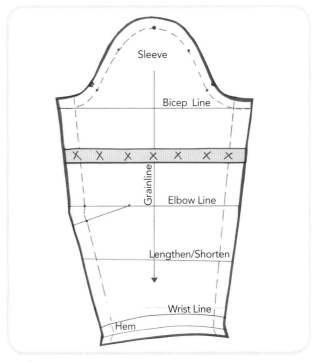

To increase

Measure down from the full bicep to the elbow. Draw a horizontal line across the pattern, approximately in the middle of this area. Cut and spread the pattern by the amount needed to increase and match your mid-arm length.

To decrease

Measure down from the full bicep to the elbow. Draw a horizontal line across the pattern approximately in the middle of this area. Cut apart and bring the upper part of the sleeve down to overlap the lower sleeve. Deduct the amount necessary to shorten the pattern and match your arm length. The Xs indicate the portion of the pattern that is being removed.

Elbow to Wrist

Have you ever heard that the length from your elbow to your wrist matches the length of your foot? For me this is true, but I don't know if it's true for everyone. What *is* true is that this third length measurement is probably one that almost every sewist has actually seen before. It is the only sleeve adjustment printed on most sewing patterns. Lengthening or shortening this area, however, will not correct the upper part of the sleeve or cap. It can only refine the part of the sleeve pattern below the elbow. This is just another reason to apply your own measurements to all areas of a pattern for creating the perfect fit.

This measurement is fluid because some people like longer sleeves and others like shorter sleeves. If you move your arms a lot, you may measure a little longer so you have that extra amount during the fitting.

Lengthening or shortening the sleeve needs to be done within the area of measure and not on the edge or bottom of the sleeve pattern. Adjusting on the bottom edge will only create an exaggerated wrist rather than increasing or decreasing length for the arm.

Measure from the elbow down to the natural wrist.

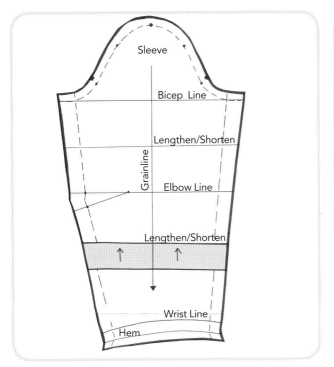

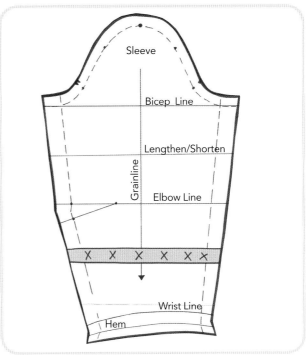

To increase

Draw a horizontal line approximately in the middle of the elbow and wrist section of the pattern. Cut on this line and spread the pattern by the amount needed to increase and match your lower arm.

To decrease

Draw a horizontal line approximately in the middle of the elbow and wrist section of the pattern. Cut apart. Overlap the bottom edge of the pattern over the upper sleeve. Cut away the amount necessary to decrease and shorten the lower arm of the sleeve. This all happens below the dart. The Xs indicate the portion of the lower sleeve that is being removed.

Tip

Of any pattern adjustment, this one has an accurate adjustment line printed on most patterns, but it only correctly adjusts the lower edge of the sleeve. This cannot help with cap fitting. Sewists mistakenly use this line to lengthen or shorten other areas of the sleeve. Remember that adjustments directly address that area of measure.

Chapter 7

Horizontal Arm Adjustments

Through common-sense application, I discovered a half cap adjustment that is a great trick for fitting the upper part of the horizontal sleeve cap. Shortly after, I started applying this technique to other areas of the sleeve when adjusting the circumference. This modification of the traditional L-slash adjustment has allowed me to work within the body of the pattern rather than just adding to the outer edge when fitting sleeves around the fullness of the arm. However, adding to the edge of the pattern is still a viable option for adjusting the horizontal measurements. The key is having options so you can find the best solutions for your fitting issues. Whether you have narrow upper arms, full biceps, forward-tilting shoulder points or any other fitting challenge, I have some new tips and tricks along with my approach to traditional pattern adjustments that you can use to easily modify the horizontal sleeve pattern.

▶▶ Advanced Measuring

Arms can be different from the front to back due to extra padding, muscle placement, lymphedema (localized swelling and fluid retention) or other reasons. You can further refine your fit and measurements by placing garment tape down the length of the arm from the shoulder point to wrist. Also mark the underarm from the armpit to the wrist (this shows the location of the underarm seam). Now you have a front and back sleeve, and you can compare measurements to see if one area is different from the other. See the advanced application tricks throughout this chapter.

Horizontal Arm
Measurement Chart

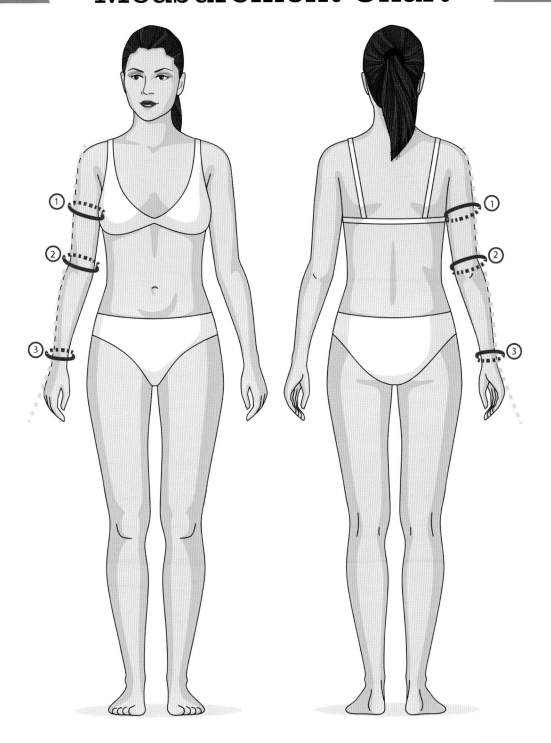

1	Bicep	
2	Elbow	
3	Wrist	

Bicep

The bicep measurement usually lines up with the full bust on the torso. On some people, however, this line can be higher or lower on the body. Simply measure what is natural for your arm.

Measure around the fullest part of the upper arm, below the shoulder point and above the elbow. Add 2" (5.1cm) to this measurement for the standard amount of movement ease necessary in sleeve fitting.

Marking Your Own Bicep Line

The bicep line is usually printed on commercial patterns. If your pattern does not have a bicep line, measure down 1" (2.5cm) from the top of the side seam of the pattern. Do this on both sides and use a ruler to connect, creating a bicep line.

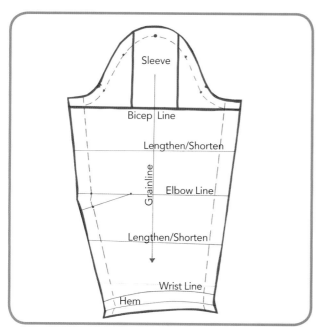

L-slash marking

The L-slash method of adjusting the full bicep is a traditional adjustment that works to easily increase and decrease the full bicep. Simply draw a vertical line on each side of the shoulder point down from the top of the pattern to the bicep line. Place the vertical lines about halfway between the center and the side of the pattern.

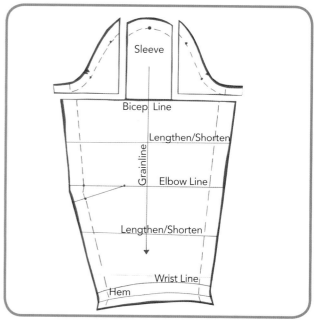

L-slash cutting

Cut across the pattern on the bicep line over to the vertical line drawn down from the top edge of the pattern. Cut on the vertical line. This creates an L-shaped cut in the pattern. Do this on both sides. You now have two movable portions of pattern that you can slide outward or inward to increase or decrease the bicep fullness.

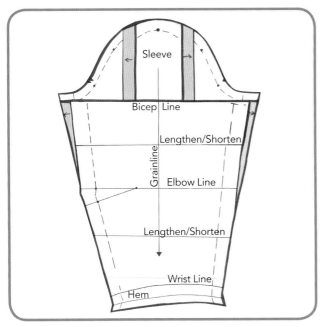

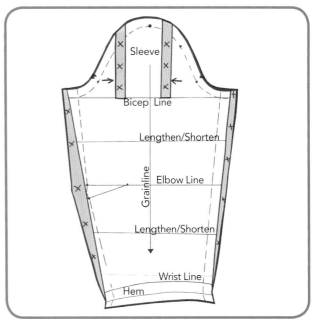

L-slash increase

Now that you have two L-shaped portions of the pattern, simply slide them outward on the bicep line to add width and increase the bicep. In this example, the amount added is divided evenly on the front and back of the pattern. Take a ruler and true up each side by gradually transitioning into the side seam of the pattern. The more you increase the bicep, the farther down the pattern you will need to taper the side seam.

L-slash decrease

To decrease the bicep and narrow the sleeve, slide the L-shaped portions of the pattern inward on the bicep lines, creating an overlap. In this example, the amount decreased is divided evenly on the front and the back of the pattern. When truing the side seams on a decrease, you will not normally angle back out, creating an odd side seam shape (although there are always exceptions). Instead, you will gently taper down the length of the sleeve until a nice line is created. The Xs indicate the portion of the pattern that is being removed.

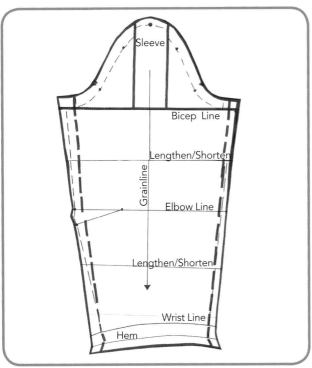

L-slash decrease trued pattern

This is the finished example of decreasing the pattern at the bicep and truing up the side seams. The solid red lines are where the L-shaped adjustments were made, and the dotted lines down the side are the new stitching lines. The pattern is much narrower due to the decrease.

 Advanced Application

The L-slash adjustment does not need to be symmetrical on the front and back of the pattern, contrary to traditional application. You may need more on one side and less on the other. You also might increase one side and decrease the other. If you have fuller arms, and that fullness happens toward the back of the arm (usually due to large padding in the bicep), you might only need to increase the back part of the pattern. Or the opposite is possible. If you have large bicep muscles or padding in the front of the arm, then increase the front of the pattern. Be flexible with the application of this adjustment.

Back Upper Half Cap

The upper half cap adjustment is not something you need to take a measurement for. Well, not exactly. This is one of the best tricks I teach. After finding that a large majority of my clients have forward-tilting shoulders, I started to notice that the upper back half of the cap of the sleeve needed that extra-special touch to make the fit even more perfect. This adjustment applies only to an increase on the back upper cap of the sleeve pattern.

A-ha moment: There is a direct correlation between prominent forward shoulder points, the elongated back sleeve cap, drag lines on the upper sleeve, comfort and how sleeves move and fit the body. Okay, that's not news to everyone, but what I started to do in my fittings was one of those "Why didn't I think of that sooner?" moments. All of these things can be fixed in a small area on the upper back of the sleeve.

Solution: Why not add to the back cap of the sleeve, but only on the top half, just to the back of the shoulder point? I knew the L-slash worked to increase the bicep, so why not use it solely on the upper back cap to lengthen the area of the pattern that normally flattens out?

The benefit is a natural sleeve shape all over the sleeve rather than only addressing the forward-tilting shoulder and hyper-fitting the back. I also found a solution to many sleeve-fitting questions that I receive quite frequently.

Most traditional methods approach fitting this area by dividing the sleeve ease evenly between the front and back and lightly fitting the slope rather than perfecting the armhole shape, which creates a more natural shape.

Tip

Very prominent collarbones can create the same fitting issues that a forward-tilting shoulder creates. So even if your arms are not forward-tilting, this adjustment might be a solution if your armhole is shifting forward.

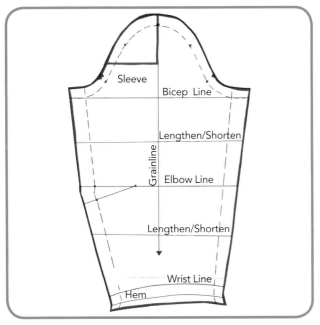

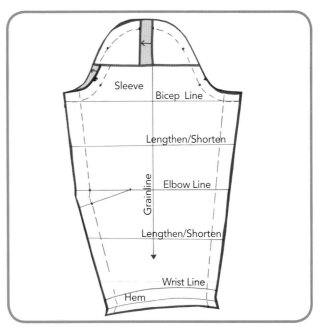

Marking

Marking your pattern for the upper half cap adjustment uses the same principle as the bicep L-slash method. On the back upper cap, measure about halfway down the center of the sleeve and then over to the edge of the pattern. This creates an L-shaped cutting line.

To increase

Simply shift the upper back cap of the pattern outward, lengthening the upper back cap. True the outer edge of the pattern. Notice we are not increasing the bicep, only the upper back of the sleeve. *Tip:* As you apply this adjustment, you can not only shift this pattern section outward to add length, but you can also shift it upward to add height. This is effective if you have very square shoulders and have a larger space to fill as you join to the torso.

Tips

- *When fitting the torso of a forward-tilting arm, do not pin out excess on the body of the back torso. Instead, place shoulder padding in the back armhole to fill out where the back normally flattens out. You do not need padding in the front because the forward tilt fills that out. You will now have an even and natural-looking armhole. Apply the back upper half cap adjustment to the sleeve and, voilà! Better shape = better sewing.*

- *How do you measure your adjustment? The height of the shoulder pad is a good indicator of how much you need to add to the pattern; however, this is fluid because there are so many armhole variations. Every time I do this adjustment, it is different, but by visually evaluating the sleeve on the fit sample, you can measure the distance where the sleeve gaps or is pulling at the back.*

- *You do not have to address this adjustment in the pattern stage. You can, but being visual, I like to fit the muslin fit sample first, fit my vertically and horizontally adjusted sleeve pattern to the fit sample and then calculate my adjustment for the cap of the pattern.*

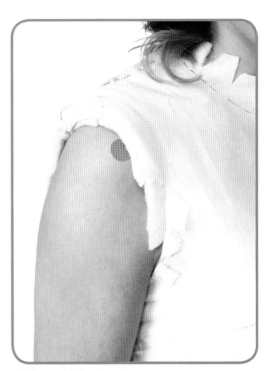

A forward-tilting shoulder.

Elbow

Many sleeve patterns have an elbow fitting dart. If you do not have an elbow line marked on your pattern, you can simply draw a horizontal line across the pattern at the top of the elbow dart. If your pattern does not have an elbow dart, you can allocate space for this by creating a line approximately in the middle of the pattern between the bicep and wrist area. Make sure to then adjust the vertical areas of the pattern according to Chapter 6 and then proceed with this width adjustment.

Sometimes you need to quickly add width to or deduct it from the midsection of the sleeve pattern. If this change is not a major alteration to the pattern, the traditional method of using the edge or side seam is simple and direct.

Measure around the elbow or fullest part of the midsection of the arm. Add 2" (5.1cm) to this measurement for the standard amount of movement ease necessary in sleeve fitting.

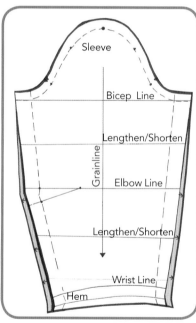

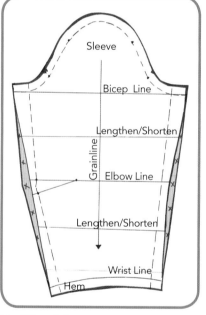

Tip

Turn to the end of this chapter to see how to apply the L-slash method to the elbow adjustment. This is a great alternative to the traditional method because it allows you to work within the body of the pattern.

Traditional increase

At the elbow line on your pattern, measure out half the amount needed to increase on both sides of the pattern. Use a ruler and transition out to the upper edge of the sleeve so you are adding only to the midsection. Transition out to the hem of the sleeve or add the same amount evenly down the sleeve. You can easily pin out excess during the muslin fitting if you want to add the fullness evenly to the hem like in this example. This example evenly divides the increase.

Traditional decrease

At the elbow line on the pattern, measure inward half the amount necessary to decrease the pattern and match your measurements. Use a ruler to transition out to the original edge on the upper part of the side seam. Because we normally do not want very narrow sleeves at the wrist, when transitioning to the hem, gradually taper out to the original hemline. You can always pin out excess during the muslin fitting if you decide to take in the wrist area. In this pattern, the decrease is divided evenly on both sides of the sleeve. The Xs indicate the portion of the pattern that is being removed.

Wrist

If you have larger upper arms, you may increase this measurement so you are not accentuating the fuller upper arm. It is always easy to pin in excess during the muslin fitting, and you do need to be able to put your hand into the garment, so it is okay to be generous when measuring the wrist.

Wrist adjustments on the pattern are done at the wristline, not at the bottom edge of the pattern. Make sure you are increasing or decreasing in the area above the seam and hem allowance.

Measure around the wrist just above the bone at the base of the thumb where the hand joins the arm. Add 2" (5.1cm) to this measurement for the standard amount of movement ease necessary in sleeve fitting.

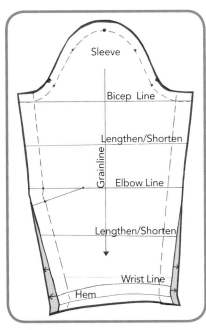

Traditional increase

At the wristline on your pattern, measure out half the amount needed to increase on both sides of the pattern. Use a ruler and transition out toward the elbow. The more you increase, the higher you will transition upward on the pattern. This example evenly divides the increase.

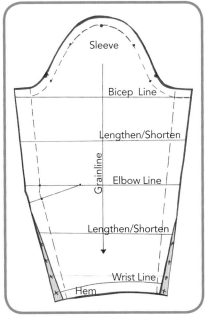

Traditional decrease

At the wristline on your pattern, measure half the amount needed to decrease on both sides of the pattern. Use a ruler and taper inward toward the elbow. The Xs indicate the portion of the pattern that is being removed. The more you decrease, the higher your transition upward on the pattern. Be careful not to create a wrist that is too narrow, as you will have difficulties putting your hand into the garment. If you want a fitted sleeve, make sure to pattern a closure opening, such as buttons and a vent.

Advanced Application

If one side of your arm is wider than the other, you can create the adjustment on a single side of the pattern, if that better replicates your arm shape, or use different amounts on each side. For example, arms with full padding on the back might require a larger increase on the back rather than dividing evenly between the front and the back.

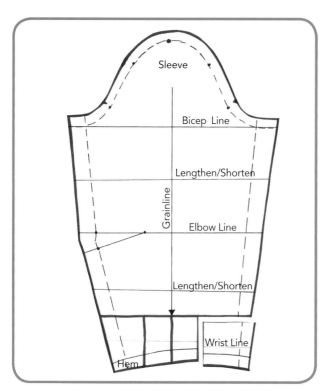

L-slash marking

The L-slash method also works well on the lower part of the sleeve. Draw a horizontal line across the sleeve approximately one half or one third of the distance from the wrist to the elbow. Mark the center of the sleeve (usually you can simply extend the grainline). Draw a vertical line up the pattern, positioned halfway between the center of the sleeve (or grainline) and the outer edge. Place a line on the front and back of the pattern. Cut up the vertical line and across the horizontal line, creating an L-shaped movable segment.

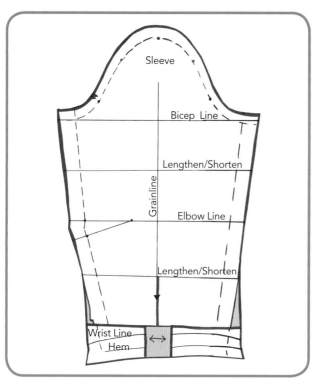

L-slash adjustment

Shift the L-shaped portion over and outward, increasing the width on the front, back or both edges of the sleeve. You can also shift the section of pattern down, creating length in just that specific area. True up the side seam by transitioning upward on the sleeve. The L-slash allows you to transition out much sooner on the sleeve, widening less area of the pattern. In this example, the front of the wrist was increased more than the back, allowing for more customizing of the pattern.

Why Use the L-Slash on the Wrist?

Some complex sleeve patterns have markings for vents, buttonholes and myriad other markings. The L-slash is a quick alternative for adjusting the elements rather than remarking all the placement lines. This is also great for addressing fullness in either the front or back independently.

Combination Sleeves and Sleeve Extras

Pattern adjustments should be easy to apply and sometimes they use creative solutions as well. The L-slash adjustment is a simple traditional solution for the bicep, and easy to apply at the wrist, but what about using the L-slash within the body of the sleeve pattern? This might be a modified sleeve solution for your pattern adjustments.

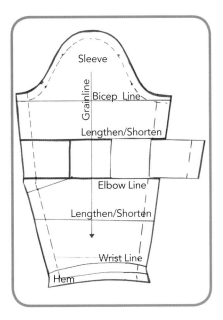

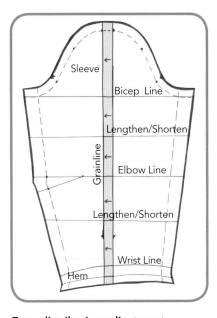

Elbow L-slash marking

Draw a horizontal line across the pattern at the top of the elbow dart and also across the pattern halfway between the elbow and bicep. You can work higher or lower on the pattern depending on your arm contours. Draw a vertical line down the center of your pattern (usually the grainline falls here). Between the two horizontal lines, draw a vertical line on each side of the sleeve halfway between the center of the sleeve and the outer edge of the sleeve. Cut across the lower horizontal line, up the vertical and back across the upper horizontal line, creating a movable section of pattern. You will have one on each side or one on a single side if you are working solely on one side of the pattern.

Elbow L-slash adjustment

Shift the movable portion of pattern outward to increase or inward to decrease the midsection of your pattern. If you need an even amount of adjustment, you can cut all the way through to the middle line as in this illustration. Truing the side seams is easy, and with this adjustment, there is little disturbance on the outer edge of the pattern.

Even distribution adjustment

Throughout this chapter we have treated each pattern refinement separately, and sleeve patterns often need adjustments in targeted areas. However, if you find you need a simple pattern increase or decrease the entire length of the pattern, you can slash right down the middle and spread or overlap the pattern the amount needed. This is a very generic distribution of pattern refinement, but it is available if you want a quick width change.

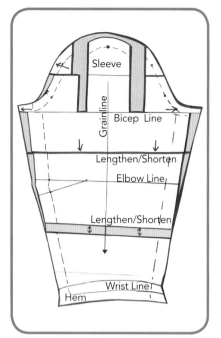

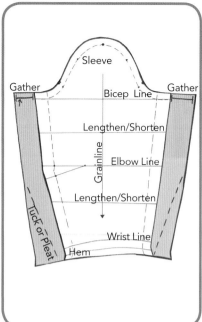

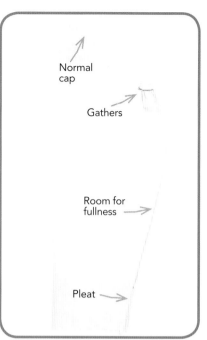

Combination example

This pattern could easily belong to any reader of this book. It looks like a lot, but in reality these pattern modifications can take less than five minutes. Let's walk though what we see here. Vertically, the sleeve needed shortening between the bicep and the elbow, and it needed lengthening below the elbow (note that you can't do both on the same line like most sewists do). Horizontally, we see the L-slash to increase the width, truing down the side seam. The back upper half cap adjustment adds extra length at the top back of the pattern. All of this in four cuts of the scissors—it really is that easy! The next step is pin fitting the cap, and you have a perfect sleeve.

Solutions for full underarms, lymphedema and the infamous "underarm waddle"

It is a fact of life that the underarm does not always stay firm. It oftentimes can get very large, which creates difficulty in patterning a sleeve. Just because you have exaggerated underarm fullness, however, does not mean you will have an exaggerated sleeve cap. You can actually fit this type of arm easily and make it look lovely on a garment.

Create a pattern to the proportion of your arm. Widen the pattern at the bicep and down the sleeve as needed. You do not want to use a ruler and connect the exaggerated bicep to the wrist, making a super-narrow wrist. This will exaggerate the issue. Evenly add fullness down the entire pattern length.

To sew, you will either gather the fullness at the bicep or create a tuck with the excess fabric at the underarm. This will sew nicely into the normal-shaped armhole, but the sleeve will open up to allow for the arm fullness. The excess is hidden at the underarm. Now the excess fullness at the wrist is easily sewn into a nice tuck or pleat partially up the seam, allowing for the sleeve to fall open at the fullest part of the arm.

Tip

Cut this type of sleeve on the bias if your fabric will allow for more stretch and movement. Seams are your friend. Creating two to three vertical seams on the sleeve will allow you to contour the sleeve around the fuller areas of the arm and transition nicely into the armhole and wrist.

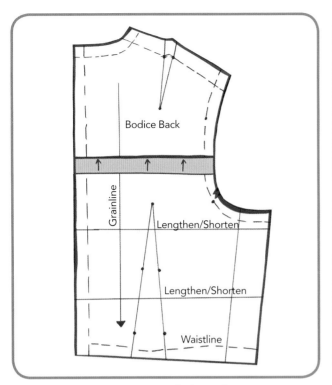

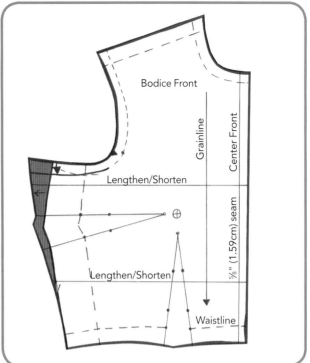

Treat sleeve patterns separately from the torso

Traditionally, sewists have been taught to apply the same vertical adjustments to a sleeve pattern that you apply to the torso when addressing length. Just because you need a pattern change on the torso, however, does not mean it always translates to the sleeve. Torso changes apply only to the torso. Sleeve changes apply to the sleeve. They still blend together easily in the muslin fitting. See Chapter 8.

Extending the underarm

If you are increasing the width of the full bust at the side seam, you do need to lengthen the bicep line on the sleeve pattern so they match. Otherwise the sleeve will be too short in the underarm.

Ease and the Polished Fit

The most enjoyable part of designing clothing and fitting for me is when I create a fit sample that is so close to my client's body that they comment in amazement that I created a pattern with an almost perfect fit—from measurements alone! I even had a college professor from a prominent fashion design department make the statement, "You can do that?" when I said I never see most of my clients in person. Yes, if you have a good set of measurements, you can make any pattern replicate a person's body pretty accurately. Fit is all about scale and proportion, not traditional generic adjustments.

In chapters 2–7, we went through many vertical and horizontal raw proportion adjustments. Think of those lessons like learning an easy custom version of pattern grading. Now all that is left is the "tweaking" or polishing of your pattern. *Always make a fit sample.* This allows you to do the polishing and make the finishing touches to fit that you need to apply visually. Fit is fun and easy if you correct fit in the pattern. It's less about drama and more about art!

All About Ease

What is ease? Similar to sleeves, ease is one of those sewing hot buttons that is made more difficult or confusing than necessary. Forget generic charts because, just like patterns, each person has their own perspective when it comes to fit. For example, what is considered semi-fitted on you might be loose-fitting on your neighbor. Keep it simple. Fit ease, or what I call "wiggle room," is the extra room above your measurements so you can bend, move and function. Design ease, or how I define "silhouette," is anything above your wiggle room. Forget formulas and numbers, because they're different on every person, and certain areas of patterns have little or no ease. The key is to recognize where ease goes on a garment.

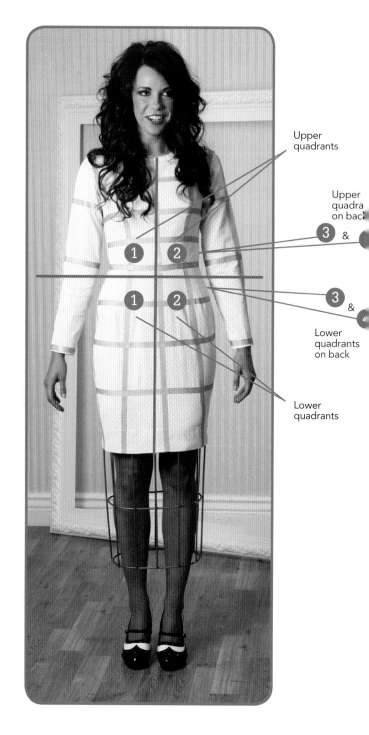

Upper quadrants

Upper quadra on bac

3 &

3 &

Lower quadrants on back

Lower quadrants

Ease guidelines

As a pattern drafter and draper, I build fit ease or "wiggle room" into my patterns. These are the only standard measurements that I follow and, even then, they can be modified. The torso and lower body are divided into quadrants; two on the front and two on the back.

Sleeves: +2" (5.1cm) horizontally
Torso: +¼"–½" (6mm–1.3cm) per quadrant
Lower Body: +½"–1" (1.3cm–2.5cm) per quadrant
Sleeve Cap Height: +¼" (6mm) or additional if adding shoulder padding

Little or no ease

Ease is not always evenly distributed throughout the pattern. As you have gone through the pattern adjustment chapters, you should have noticed that you measured the body and directly applied these measurements to the pattern. Some areas of fit use a literal translation and need little to no ease added to the body measurement on the pattern. Making these areas of the pattern bigger will defeat the purpose of customizing the pattern and trying to replicate your body proportion. Unless there is a silhouette or design reason to not replicate the body, some of the main areas where you do not need to add ease include the following:

> Most vertical measurements
> Shoulder to apex
> Bust curve
> Apex to apex
> Other areas related to close-fitting garments

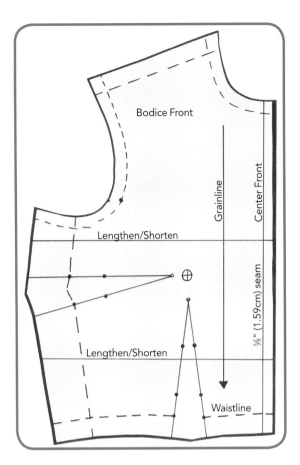

Some areas of a pattern require little to no ease or an exact comparison to body measurements. This will often apply to most vertical measurements or areas related to close-fitting garments.

When ease intersects details

Consider design details when applying ease. For example, a shirt with a button front needs to lie nicely over the bust area without too much excess creating a baggy front. Other things, like collars and lapels, also need to lie flat without excess. These are just a few examples showing why some areas of a pattern need to reflect the body measurements exactly in order for design details to lay correctly.

Silhouette and customizable ease

Everybody has their own interpretation when it comes to comfort in clothing and just how much room they truly need. It also varies on different garment styles, and this is why generic charts rarely apply. Often people need less of this extra fullness than they think, and it is often less than what is included in many commercial patterns. You can have a loose-fitting garment that is still tailored attractively without having too much fullness that creates a sloppy fit.

After eliminating portions of the pattern that do not need excess ease, you can now increase your pattern in the remaining areas. Because your pattern is now in the correct proportion of your body, you will find that most silhouette ease happens off center and more toward the side of the garment (unless a style calls for something different).

How do you know how much add?

› Apply extra on top of body measurements and "wiggle room" ease.
› Evaluate pattern side areas that are not within design details or fitting elements.
› If you have too much excess, you can always pin fit this out during the muslin fitting without disturbing the proportion of the pattern.
› Chapter 9 gives examples of various garments and their ease.

Unfitted
An unfitted or loose-fitted garment is not necessarily sloppy in fit, but extra ease around the garment creates a more casual and comfortable fit.

Fitted
Fitted garments measure larger than the body, but only enough so they do not appear baggy or unfitted.

Very fitted
The very fitted garment closely follows the contour of the body. Be careful not to over-fit on woven garments. They still need some wiggle room or a small amount of ease to prevent pulling or a too-tight fit.

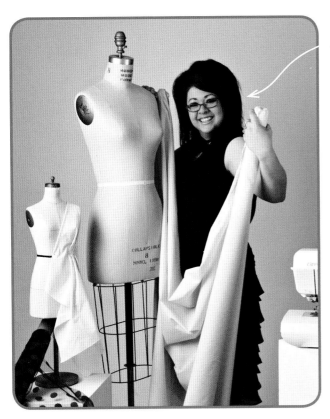

Joi's selfie.

Fabrics and ease

As you consider fitting and silhouette ease while fitting your muslin sample, you also want to think about the final fashion fabric. Heavier fabrics may require more ease, depending on the style of garment, while fabrics woven with stretch fibers might allow for a closer fit while still being comfortable. The best fitters combine fabric characteristics with fitting principles to make the best decisions on how much excess is necessary for a polished look. Also note that, as you layer garments, the farther away they are from the body, the more ease they will need to allow for a proper fit over other pieces. It is always much easier to take in than it is to let out!

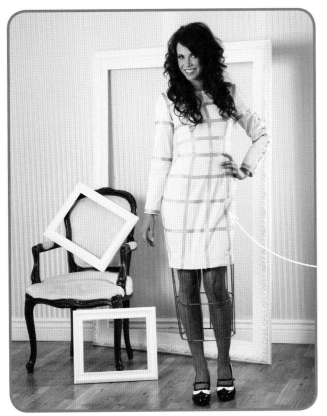

Recognizing movement

Learn to recognize movement in fabric and motion. Part of fitting is learning to decipher the difference between fit issues and natural movement in a garment due to the motion of the body and characteristics of the fabric. Fitting while standing perfectly still looks great, but understand that you won't be holding a model pose continually. Be realistic about how you expect some fabrics to perform and what movement will do to a garment.

Movement lines
are not fit issues.

Sewing a Fit Sample

Up to this point, you have adjusted your pattern vertically and then horizontally to replicate your own body proportion and possibly modified the ease for comfort and design. "Measure yourself, measure your pattern" is a quick, fluid and efficient method that corrects almost all fit issues with raw proportional changes to the pattern. All that's left is polishing the fit and fine-tuning on your fit sample. No more fit anxiety!

1. Sew a fit sample from muslin cloth or something similar in weight and texture to the final garment.
2. Your fit sample should be the basic garment pieces basted together. Omit details like pockets, buttons, etc.
3. Some sewists fit with the seam allowance facing outward, but I prefer pressing my seams and having them toward the inside. You choose what method visually works best for you.
4. Mark and write directly on your fit sample. This is where the perfecting happens.
5. This will be your new pattern.

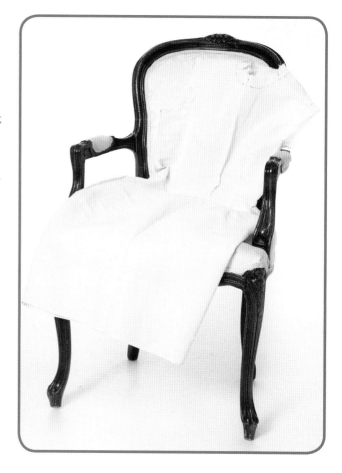

Prepping the body: Foundations and fit

Expert fitters understand the importance of correct undergarments. What you have on underneath directly reflects how a garment looks on the outside, and this structure is key to a great fit. Wear undergarments that are appropriate for your specific clothing.

For example, if you're wearing a loose sweater, you might be okay with a sports bra and your everyday skivvies, but if you are wearing a formal gown, you need briefs that create a nice hip curve with no panty indentations, you might need a longline bra or something with more structure, and you might also need to wear a slip or body shaper. The combinations are limitless; however, be reasonable and realistic. You can't expect a perfect fit if your undergarments are not cooperating.

Don't forget to fit your garment wearing the correct shoes too. Your posture is affected by the height of your shoes, and that can modify the hang of your clothing.

Remember, the body is a moving object, and we don't always notice the daily fluctuations in our everyday stretchy undergarments. Correct foundation garments create a consistency in what the pliable body is doing. Foundation garments do not necessarily have to be ugly or uncomfortable.

Garment contouring: Create a natural shape

Don't pin to the defect. Pinning your garment so it directly mimics your body may only accentuate body and fitting issues. Instead, even out the body. Ideally you would have done this prior to measuring so your pattern will incorporate the changes. Doing this also creates more natural garment shapes and ease in sewing. Below are just a few of the areas that you might need to contour and balance.

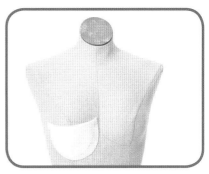

Bust cups

Bra cups can be placed on all four bust quadrants: the top of the breast (great if you sag), toward the side (perfect for filling in space), toward the center front (creates a nice foundation for center front details) and the traditional under-the-bust area. A cup under the bust can lift a breast, add fullness or help create a better foundation.

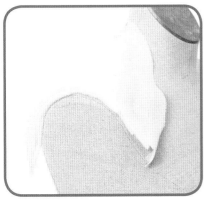

Shoulder pad

Shoulder pads are recognizable to sewists. These tools have gotten a bad rap, and many people are hesitant to consider them; however, they are not necessarily for bulk and height. Think of them as body shapers. You want to shape the body to make it look even and natural, and the shoulder area is a key fitting area because most garments hang from the shoulders and neck. It is common to have one shoulder higher or longer than the other, and simple padding can even that out. Try it and you'll love the results, because they are often very slimming. Having trouble fitting your sleeves? Check your shoulders first.

Back shoulder

Padding the upper back shoulder is necessary when you have a forward-tilting arm or simply to fill in a hollow space in the back.

Chest pads

A hollow space on the front chest is a common issue due to things such as forward-tilting shoulders, larger breasts, narrow upper chests and larger arms. Padding this area gives your garment support and a place to rest. Sleeveless garments can be padded by simply lining the garment and sewing the padding to the lining or using a matching-colored fleece.

Where to Sew Padding

Body contouring and padding may or may not be sewn into the garment. On tailored or semi-tailored garments, you might attach padding to the lining or the inside seams. However, you would not want to sew padding on garments made of knits, as it would be visible. Instead, sew the padding to a separate foundation. Sew padding on the inside of a foundation piece, such as a fitted cami or tank top that hugs the body, and you have a seamless solution to evening out the body. Simply wear the garment over the top. What you have on underneath directly affects how a garment looks on the outside.

The Fitting

The unpinned fit sample

The following process is what I do for all of my clients. Think of this as spending time in my studio and getting in on my thought process.

This sample is proportionally correct, but it needs polishing. Note what issues I am evaluating or looking for.

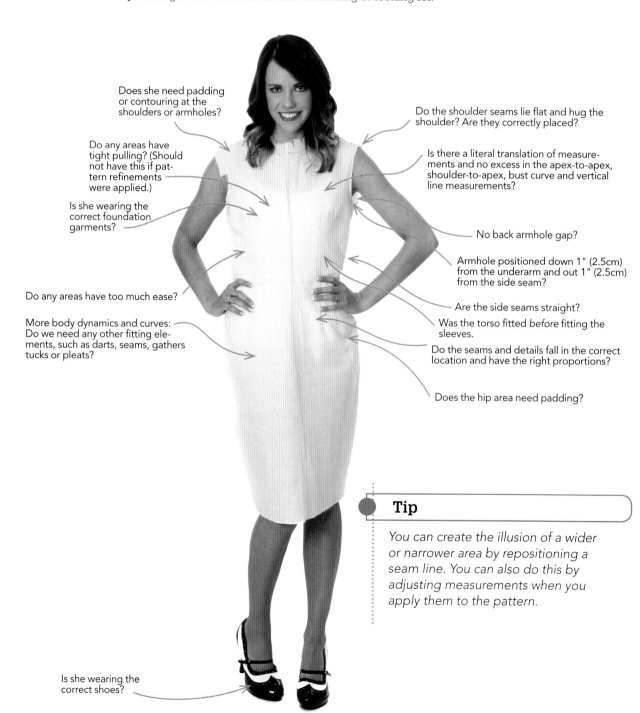

Does she need padding or contouring at the shoulders or armholes?

Do any areas have tight pulling? (Should not have this if pattern refinements were applied.)

Is she wearing the correct foundation garments?

Do any areas have too much ease?

More body dynamics and curves: Do we need any other fitting elements, such as darts, seams, gathers tucks or pleats?

Do the shoulder seams lie flat and hug the shoulder? Are they correctly placed?

Is there a literal translation of measurements and no excess in the apex-to-apex, shoulder-to-apex, bust curve and vertical line measurements?

No back armhole gap?

Armhole positioned down 1" (2.5cm) from the underarm and out 1" (2.5cm) from the side seam?

Are the side seams straight?

Was the torso fitted *before* fitting the sleeves.

Do the seams and details fall in the correct location and have the right proportions?

Does the hip area need padding?

Is she wearing the correct shoes?

> ### Tip
>
> *You can create the illusion of a wider or narrower area by repositioning a seam line. You can also do this by adjusting measurements when you apply them to the pattern.*

The polished fit sample

Working top to bottom and front to back, I have pinned all the little details that will create an impeccable fit. See how the fitting is perfecting and polishing? You can mark all of your refinements and take this directly to the fashion fabric as your final pattern, feeling confident in the fit. Once your pin fitting is complete, evaluate how the garment feels. You can visually adjust fit, but the garment has to function for the individual.

Take a look at the things I polished on this fit sample. See the next few pages for more details on individual adjustments.

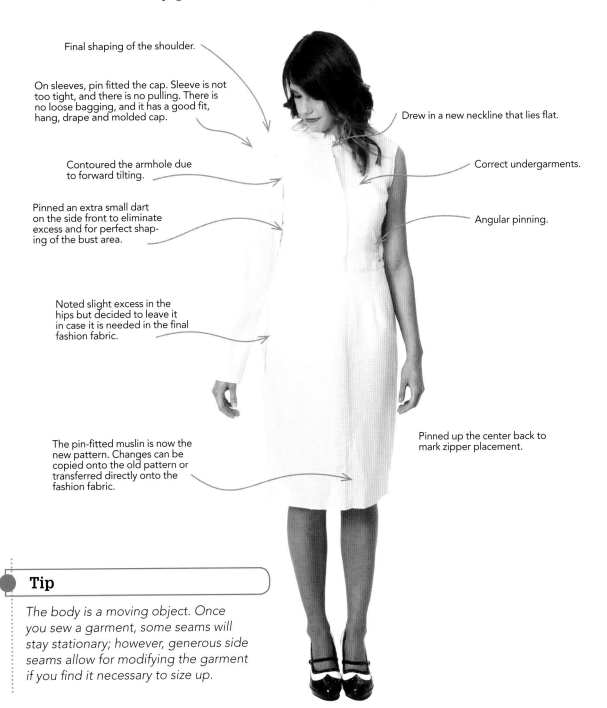

Final shaping of the shoulder.

On sleeves, pin fitted the cap. Sleeve is not too tight, and there is no pulling. There is no loose bagging, and it has a good fit, hang, drape and molded cap.

Contoured the armhole due to forward tilting.

Pinned an extra small dart on the side front to eliminate excess and for perfect shaping of the bust area.

Noted slight excess in the hips but decided to leave it in case it is needed in the final fashion fabric.

The pin-fitted muslin is now the new pattern. Changes can be copied onto the old pattern or transferred directly onto the fashion fabric.

Drew in a new neckline that lies flat.

Correct undergarments.

Angular pinning.

Pinned up the center back to mark zipper placement.

Tip

The body is a moving object. Once you sew a garment, some seams will stay stationary; however, generous side seams allow for modifying the garment if you find it necessary to size up.

Forward-tilting shoulder

A shoulder that tilts forward throws off the sleeve fit. Sleeves often pull from the back or flatten out while gapping in the front. By padding the front, you fill out the hollow area, and by placing a thin pad in the back, you create an artificial but more natural armhole, thus eliminating most, if not all, adjustments.

Final sleeve placement

After the shoulder and armhole shaping is complete, you can pin fit the cap of the sleeve onto the muslin. Always fit the torso first and then join the sleeve for a carefree fit.

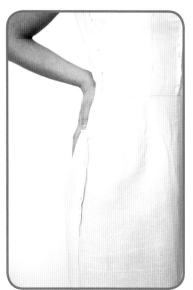

Polishing the hip curve

Because you treat the front separately from the back, you might have different hip curves on your patterns. Remember, the adjustments are *raw* proportional changes, and polishing will be needed at the fitting stage. Simply baste the side seams together, then pin the final seam around the contour of the body. Remember, some ease is necessary. Do not over-pin.

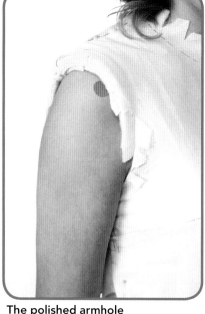

The polished armhole

The final fitted armhole will have any necessary padding, creating the correct shape, as well as clips to relax the fabric around the contours of the arm.

Neckline shaping

During your muslin fitting, you will clip the neckline so it lies flat on the body. The fit sample has a high neckline that hugs the base of the neck. You will want a close fit if you are adding a collar. Otherwise, take a marking pen and draw in the desired shape of your finished neckline. Baste around the marking before cutting to prevent stretching the neckline and to ensure a close fit next to the body.

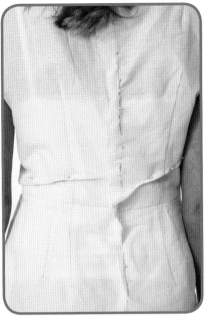

Eliminating extra fabric

Often, small amounts of fabric fall between seams. This excess fabric can be vertical, horizontal or angular. Simply pin within the pattern piece to grade out the extra. This will not be a seam, dart or anything else. Baste across the excess, remove your pins, and when you cut your garment or final pattern, treat the excess fabric as if it's not even there.

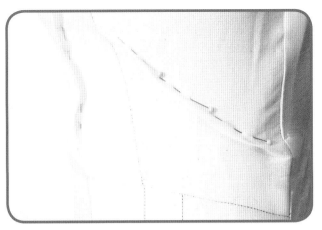

Angular pinning

When I remove excess fabric from within a pattern piece and it falls at an angle, I call it angular pinning. This is one of my best fitting tips because many people only pin at the seams. This does not result in a flat, tailored look. Angular pinning is one of those final polishing tricks that has to be done at the muslin fit stage. You cannot address this in a flat pattern, and that is why it's necessary to create a fit sample for any garment you are sewing.

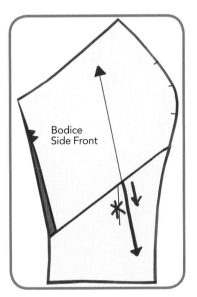
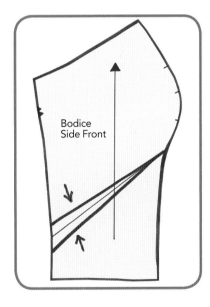

Triple bust marking

When marking princess seams around the apex area, patterns normally only have one notch on the bust curve. However, I place three notches on the curve: one above, one below and one on the apex. This allows me to perfectly match up and ease in the longer pattern piece exactly.

Garment Application Workbook

How do you apply body measurements and pattern adjustments to a variety of garment styles?

In this chapter, I will introduce you to a variety of garment styles and help you learn to recognize certain measurements that are relevant to those particular types of garments. Of course, there is no limit to garments that we can illustrate, but it's not necessary to cover them all, either. After walking through a few examples, you will find the process of evaluating a garment and choosing the specific areas of measure easy and efficient. Not every area of measure is necessary for every type of garment, thus simplifying the method.

Using Your Fit Pattern With a Fashion Pattern

The fit pattern used to illustrate this process is not an actual fashion garment pattern. It is like a worksheet to help you practice fitting methods. However, some sewists ask how they can use the perfected fit pattern along with their fashion patterns. It really is not necessary once you learn the "measure yourself, measure your pattern" method since it works on any pattern, but here is what you do if you want to use the fitting from your fit sample. In this example, we will walk through a front bodice pattern.

1. Select a fashion pattern close to your size.
This is a starting point for the style of garment. Don't get hung up on size since we are using the correct fittings from your fit sample. Cut out the fashion pattern pieces necessary for the garment. You can leave the seam allowance or trim it off. If you cut it off, remember to add it once your pattern is complete.

2. Compare the vertical fit on both patterns.
Line up the apex on both patterns. The fit pattern will have your correct fitted lengths from the shoulder to apex, bust curve and underbust to waist. These are literal translations of your body. If there is extra length on the fashion pattern, you have to decide if that is necessary for the silhouette and style of the garment, or if you should deduct and use the correct heights on your fit pattern. If the fit pattern is longer than the fashion pattern, you definitely need to use the fit pattern lengths so it will fit your body.

3. Compare the horizontal fit on both patterns.
Various garments have variations in fullness, according to our chapter on ease, and this will be unique from person to person. If the fashion pattern is smaller than your fit sample, you know the garment pattern needs to be at least as full around as the fit pattern and possibly bigger, depending on the style. In this case, adding might be necessary. If the garment pattern is bigger than your fit pattern, then you know there is design ease in the garment. You can add more to make it bigger, if necessary, but you know it will go around the body.

Finishing

There is no set formula for how much to add above the fit sample in order to be a certain style. Because garment styles and body types are unlimited, the key is to learn to evaluate the pattern. Remember, many garments fit larger than the body, and garments get larger as you start to layer them over each other. If you have a little excess, it is easy to pin out during a fitting. Most importantly, the fashion pattern needs to be at least as big as the fit sample.

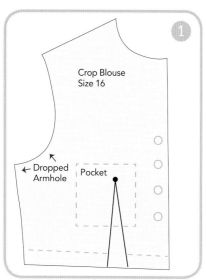
Select a fashion pattern close to your size.

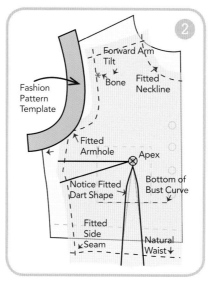
Compare the vertical fit on both patterns.

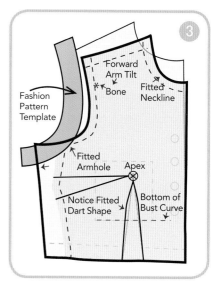
Compare the horizontal fit on both patterns.

The Boxy Jacket

Key measurements:

- ☐ Shoulder to apex
- ☐ Bust curve
- ☐ Underbust to waist
- ☐ Cap height
- ☐ Sleeve length sections (bicep to elbow, elbow to wrist)
- ☐ Apex to apex
- ☐ Apex to side seam
- ☐ Full upper back (shoulders)
- ☐ Shoulder length (although this may be made much longer for styling)

Fitting description:

This is a common silhouette for many garment styles. The fit is loose, and the cut is square or rectangular. Fitting elements often include a minimal side bust dart or no dart at all. The garment can be tailored but does not hug the body.

Ease:

Vertical measurements may reflect the body literally, while horizontal measurements will have more design ease on top of the body measurements. Areas like the apex to apex will still match the body closely to avoid throwing off the proportion in that area of fit.

Related styles:

- ⟩ Blouse
- ⟩ Coat
- ⟩ Bolero
- ⟩ Loosely tailored jacket
- ⟩ Loose-fitting empire dress

Pea Coat

Tailored Suit Jacket

Cropped Jacket with Zipper Front

The Classic Blouse

Fitted Blouse with Details

Baby-Doll Top

Shirt with Peplum

Key measurements:

- ☐ Shoulder to apex
- ☐ Bust curve
- ☐ Underbust to waist
- ☐ Cap height
- ☐ Sleeve length sections (bicep to elbow, elbow to wrist)
- ☐ Apex to apex
- ☐ Apex to side seam
- ☐ Front waist
- ☐ Back waist
- ☐ Full upper back (shoulders)
- ☐ Shoulder length
- ☐ For designs with princess seams: Center front waist to lower vertical bustline

Fitting description:

A perfectly fitted and proportional blouse is essential in any wardrobe. It is very versatile, and you can never have too many in different colors, fabrics and patterns. A blouse can be tailored to loosely fit your body without looking sloppy if certain areas of the pattern replicate your body correctly. Your blouse pattern may only have a side bust dart, or it might incorporate princess seams or waist darts.

Ease:

Vertical measurements may reflect the body literally, while horizontal measurements will have more design ease on top of the body measurements. Areas like the apex to apex will still match the body closely to avoid throwing off the proportion in that area of fit.

Related styles:

- ❭ Long tunic
- ❭ Boxy coat
- ❭ Loosely tailored jacket

Princess Seam Bodice

Key measurements:

- ☐ Shoulder to apex
- ☐ Bust curve
- ☐ Underbust to waist
- ☐ Apex to apex
- ☐ Apex to side seam
- ☐ Center front waist to lower vertical bustline
- ☐ Front waist
- ☐ Back waist
- ☐ Center back waist to back vertical line
- ☐ Full upper back (shoulders)

Fitting description:

A princess seam is a seam that goes over the apex. It can originate at the shoulder, armhole, side seam or waist. Princess-cut torso designs fit any figure type and are great for customizing a pattern. The vertical seam lines are not only flattering; they also provide another fitting element to tailor a garment over any curve. The pattern allows the sewist to use more areas of measure on the body, providing another level of accurate fit.

Ease:

Vertical measurements may reflect the body literally. Horizontal measurements also translate literally in this fitted design. Areas like the apex to apex will still match the body closely so as to avoid throwing off the proportion in that area of fit. To provide more room and a looser fitting design, add more ease off center and farther toward the side seam or on the side front area of the pattern.

Related styles:

❯ Tailored princess jacket
❯ Fitted coat
❯ Vest
❯ Fitted dress

Bustier

Empire Bodice

Cami Top

Shorts and Pants

Key measurements:

- ☐ Front waist
- ☐ Back waist
- ☐ Center front to lower vertical waistline (your darts, pleats or seams should fall here)
- ☐ Center back to vertical waistline
- ☐ Center front to side seam at hips
- ☐ Center back to side seam at hips
- ☐ Waist to hips at side seam
- ☐ Center front waist to abdomen
- ☐ Waist to hips (all measurements)
- ☐ Waist to hem

Fitting description:

You can easily apply the "measure yourself, measure your pattern" method to any pants or shorts pattern. Although pants have legs, the principle is the same. Measure your pant legs similar to measuring for sleeves.

Ease:

Vertical measurements may reflect the body literally, while horizontal measurements will have more design ease on top of the body measurements. Think of pants like sleeves in that you need a generic amount of required ease in order to bend and move. This is usually at least 2" (5.1cm) around the full-ness of the body. You can always pin in excess if you have too much fullness.

Related styles:

❯ Yoga pants

❯ Jeans

❯ Rompers

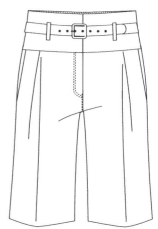

Three-quarter Khaki Pants

Jean Shorts

Tailored Shorts

A-Line Gored Skirt

Key measurements:

- ☐ Front waist
- ☐ Back waist
- ☐ Center front waist to lower vertical bustline
- ☐ Center back waist to back vertical line
- ☐ Center front to side seam at hipline
- ☐ Center back to side seam at hipline
- ☐ Waist to hips at side seam
- ☐ Waist to hips (all measurements)
- ☐ Waist to hem

Fitting description:

This is my favorite garment to make! Not everyone looks good in pants, but a correctly fitting A-line skirt with gores in it can make anyone look slimmer, taller and tailored while being comfortable. Plus, you can create many different looks with various fabrics, from denim to silk. Not every panel in a gored skirt will be symmetrical, like in commercial patterns. Measuring the body allows you to fit the body or camouflage areas of the body by adjusting where the seam lines fall on the curves.

Ease:

Vertical measurements may reflect the body literally, although past the hipline you only have length and no ease. The waist should be fitted close to the body so the garment will hang correctly and not fall off or be too tight. Due to the gored design, the skirt will gradually taper out, and the style will have ease built in.

Related styles:

- ❯ A-line skirt
- ❯ Fitted skirt
- ❯ Long skirt

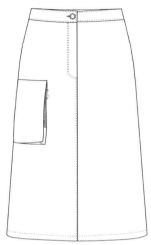

Center Front Seam Denim Skirt

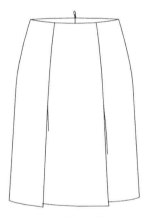

Gored Wrap Skirt

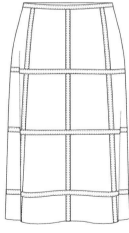

Long Fitted Skirt

Princess Line Dress

Key measurements:

- ☐ Shoulder to apex
- ☐ Bust curve
- ☐ Underbust to waist (this can stop at the waist or continue into the skirt)
- ☐ Waist to hips (on fitted styles, all measurements)
- ☐ Waist to hem
- ☐ Apex to apex
- ☐ Apex to side seam
- ☐ Front waist
- ☐ Back waist
- ☐ Center front waist to lower vertical bustline
- ☐ Full upper back (shoulders)

Fitting description:

Similar to the gored skirt, a princess dress uses vertical seams that allow you to create a more tailored garment that can be loose to snug in fit. The dress can have continuous pattern pieces from the torso over the lower body, or you can use horizontal seams at the natural waist, dropped waist or just below the bust as an empire seam. By adjusting the placement of certain lines, this is another garment that can look great on almost everybody. The key is correct proportion in your pattern. (This style is great for concealing full hips.)

Ease:

Vertical measurements may reflect the body literally, while horizontal measurements will have more design ease on top of the body measurements. This is not a tight-fitting dress, so there is excess on top of the body measurements, yet it is still well tailored. Areas like the apex to apex will match the body closely to avoid throwing off the proportion in that area of fit. The hip area has a generous amount of built-in ease due to the full skirt.

Related styles:

- ⟩ Tunic
- ⟩ Baby-doll dress
- ⟩ Beach cover-up
- ⟩ Overalls dress

Princess Seam Dress with Gathered Skirt

Empire Seam Dress

Loose-Fitting Casual Dress

Garment Style
The Princess Coat

Key measurements:

- ☐ Shoulder to apex
- ☐ Bust curve
- ☐ Underbust to waist (this can stop at the waist or continue into the skirt)
- ☐ Waist to hem
- ☐ Apex to apex
- ☐ Apex to side seam
- ☐ Front waist
- ☐ Back waist
- ☐ Center front waist to lower vertical bustline
- ☐ Full upper back (shoulders)
- ☐ Shoulder length
- ☐ Cap height
- ☐ Arm measurements (all vertical and horizontal measurements)

Fitting description:

The princess coat uses vertical seams that allow you to create a more tailored garment that can be loose to snug in fit. The coat can have continuous pattern pieces from the torso over the lower body, or you can use horizontal seams at the natural waist or dropped waist. Because this is a coat, the fit will be more spacious and have more silhouette ease in some horizontal measurements. You may incorporate a little vertical ease as well, allowing for a slightly larger garment all over.

Ease:

Vertical measurements may reflect the body literally, while horizontal measurements will have more design ease on top of the body measurements. Areas like the apex to apex will still match the body closely to avoid throwing off the proportion in that area of fit.

Related styles:
- 〉 Princess dress
- 〉 Circle-skirt dress
- 〉 Tailored jacket

Waist-Length Pea Coat

Three-Quarter Jacket

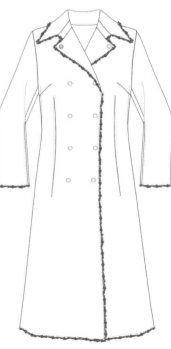

Full-Length Trench Coat

Everyday Dress

Key measurements:

- ☐ Shoulder to apex
- ☐ Bust curve
- ☐ Underbust to waist (this can stop at the waist or continue into the skirt)
- ☐ Waist to hem
- ☐ Apex to apex
- ☐ Apex to side seam
- ☐ Front waist
- ☐ Back waist
- ☐ Center front waist to lower vertical bustline
- ☐ Full upper back (shoulders)
- ☐ Shoulder length

Fitting description:

A-line to full circle-skirt dresses are almost timeless in fashion. By changing the fabrics and small details, this garment can be adapted to any time period. The fit of the torso or bodice is usually either snug or roomy, but not sloppy or baggy. There is typically a waist seam and a fitted to full skirt.

Ease:

Vertical measurements may reflect the body literally, while horizontal measurements will have more design ease on top of the body measurements with the skirt ranging from fitted to very full and roomy. Areas like the apex to apex will still match the body closely to avoid throwing off the proportion in that area of fit.

Related styles:

❭ Princess dress
❭ Circle-skirt dress
❭ Tailored jacket

Knit Dress with Gathered Skirt

Surplice-Neck Wrap Dress

Sheath Dress

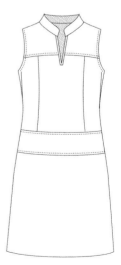

Fitted Casual Dress

Garment Style
The Coat Dress

Key measurements:

- ☐ Shoulder to apex
- ☐ Bust curve
- ☐ Underbust to waist (this can stop at the waist or continue into the skirt)
- ☐ Waist to hem
- ☐ Apex to apex
- ☐ Apex to side seam
- ☐ Front waist
- ☐ Back waist
- ☐ Center front waist to lower vertical bustline
- ☐ Full upper back (shoulders)
- ☐ Shoulder length
- ☐ Cap height
- ☐ Arm measurements (all vertical and horizontal measurements)

Fitting description:

This coat dress uses vertical seams that allow you to create a more tailored garment that is snug in fit. The coat can have continuous pattern pieces from the torso over the lower body, or you can use horizontal seams at the natural waist or dropped waist. Because this is a statement piece, the fit is tailored, and the garment is meant to be worn over lighter garments. (This style is great for concealing full hips.)

Trench Coat

Ease:

Vertical measurements will reflect the body literally, and horizontal measurements on the torso also closely match the body. The skirt is circular in cut, allowing for fullness around the lower body curves. Areas like the apex to apex will still match the body closely to avoid throwing off the proportion in that area of fit.

Related styles:

- ❭ Princess dress
- ❭ Circle-skirt dress
- ❭ Tailored jacket

Semi-Fitted Three-Quarter Coat Dress

Three-Quarter Spring Jacket Dress

The Ball Gown

Key measurements:

☐ Shoulder to apex

☐ Bust curve

☐ Underbust to waist (this can stop at the waist or continue into the skirt)

☐ Waist to hem

☐ Apex to apex

☐ Apex to side seam

☐ Front waist

☐ Back waist

☐ Center front waist to lower vertical bustline

Fitting description:

There is something special about creating a ball gown or formal gown as a wedding or event design. Often, the garment will have a fitted bodice and a very full skirt. Because the skirt is full, the only considerations are the waist-to-floor length and the correct shoes. The torso will be fitted very close by literally applying the body measurements to the pattern. Correct undergarments are key in a ball gown or evening-wear design.

Ease:

Vertical measurements will reflect the body literally, and horizontal measurements will also closely match the body measurements. Little ease is necessary in a fitted formal gown. Areas like the apex to apex will still match the body closely to avoid throwing off the proportion in that area of fit. To create illusion on the body, you can adjust the placement of the seam lines to make the bust area look wider or narrower.

Related styles:

〉Ballerina dress

〉Bustier

〉Very tailored jacket

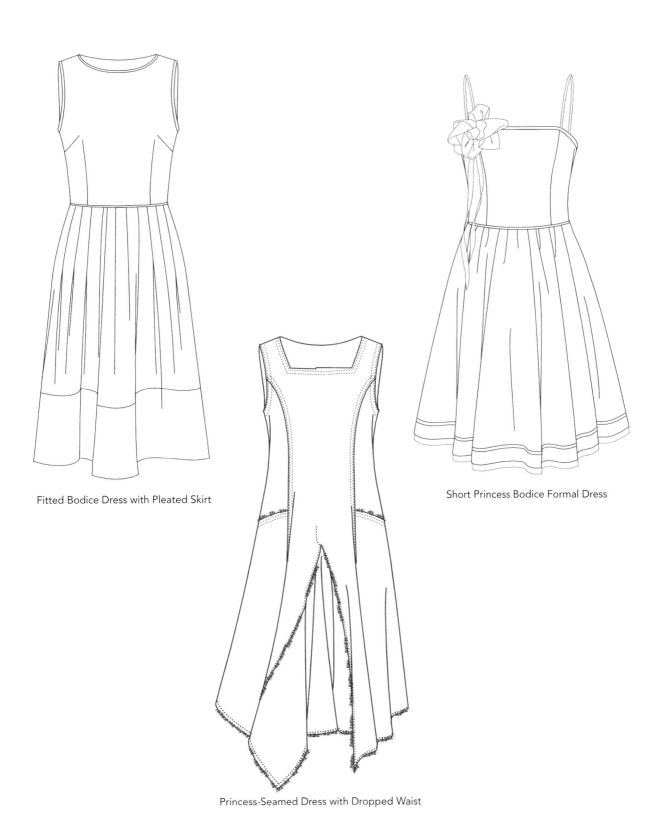

Fitted Bodice Dress with Pleated Skirt

Princess-Seamed Dress with Dropped Waist

Short Princess Bodice Formal Dress

Chapter 10

Real Bodies, Real Fit

In this final chapter, some of my friends, family, students and clients have graciously allowed me to dissect photographs of them wearing their fit samples to illustrate how the "measure yourself, measure your pattern" process aids in mastering fit.

New ideas sound great, but if you're like me, you want to see what's real! What I want you to take from this is that these are real people with real fitting needs. I took their measurements and made quick pattern adjustments to scale a pattern to their individual body types. I did not use every adjustment on every person, only what was necessary for that particular person. Polishing the pattern is still required, but you will see that the final pinning usually involves tweaking a dart or a seam, or deciding the final placement of a waistline. Fit really is that easy.

Same Pattern on Different Bodies

It is interesting to see how a fit pattern looks different on various body types. It is not meant to be a fashion garment, and even if you would not normally wear this style of garment, you can still use a fit sample in your fitting and sewing. While it is impossible to feature every fit issue, because the combinations are unlimited, it is also not necessary. By following the "measure yourself, measure your pattern" method (and perhaps adding a little body contouring), you can custom fit a pattern to your own body and truly master fit in an easy and approachable fashion.

I used a woman's size-12 fit pattern to create a fit example for everyone in this chapter—even my 10-year-old! I wanted to illustrate that a pattern is just a starting point. You can take a size 2 and scale it to a 22 if needed. No one pattern will match your entire body perfectly, so don't get stuck in that mind-set. Ideally, you want to start with a pattern that is close to your body measurements, but it doesn't have to be spot on.

I select torso patterns based on the full bust, unless the chest is dramatically larger, and lower body patterns based on full hips. As you now know, these are starting points. By simply measuring and comparing your body measurements, you can change any part of any pattern. What I also find interesting is that some areas of the size-12 pattern fit each of my volunteers exactly, no matter their size, but this is true of anyone with any pattern. This further illustrates my point of never getting hung up on pattern size.

Quirky Fitting Issues

When you listen to how other people describe their own unique figure variations, you realize that no one is perfect, no matter what size they are. Here are some quotes from some sewing friends and students:

I am a very elongated triangle. My boyfriend commented that I am shaped like a Christmas tree. He meant well. —Sue

I am more like a paper doll: flat everywhere with broad shoulders and hips. —Rachel

I have a love-hate relationship with my bust. Proper fitting techniques have helped me to complement my shape, and my bust is no longer the bane of my existence. —Khristal

My body is like dressing a sack of potatoes. —Dru

I have tree trunks for legs. —Lauren

I am a barrel with toothpicks for legs. —Anonymous

My mom has a tiny French physique; I think I inherited the chubby Dutch from my dad. —Guess who

I am like fitting a potato rather than a vase. —Susan

Grammy V (aka "Little Grandma")

Body description:

I have a small frame and, as I have aged, finding clothing that fits has become more difficult. Nothing ever fits my waist. I am hipless and most skirts nowadays are made without a built-in waistband. Whose idea was that? I have had rounded shoulders all my life, as did my mother and sisters, so finding stylish shirts and blouses is next to impossible.

Fun facts:

⟩ Grammy V is Joi's pocket-sized mom.

⟩ I am not a good seamstress. I have enjoyed sewing, but I am not good at it.

⟩ I tried to make a sock doll for my youngest daughter. It was comical, and I never did finish it. I gave it to her to make for her daughter, but I'm not sure if it got done. You'll have to ask her. She's the author of this book.

⟩ I am known for my amazing baking skills.

Things I like to wear:

⟩ I love skirts of all kinds, but my very favorites are free-flowing four-gored skirts. They are very comfortable.

⟩ I like A-line dresses, but good luck with that one for my body type. They just don't make dresses for normal people. I can't remember the last time I had a dress that fit well off the rack. I'm so lucky I know someone who sews and fits!

⟩ My favorite blouses are form-fitted at the waist, with long sleeves and a single button closure at the cuff.

Pattern adjustments:

☐ (Vertical) Underbust to waist decrease 1" (2.5cm) (almost a perfect vertical size 12)

☐ (Horizontal) Apex to apex decrease 1½" (3.8cm) (size 12 width is way too big across the front bust)

☐ (Horizontal) Apex to side seam decrease 1" (2.5cm)

☐ (Horizontal) Front waist increase 1" (2.5cm)

☐ (Vertical) Center front waist to hips decrease 2" (5.1cm)

☐ (Vertical) Center back waist to hips decrease 2" (5.1cm) (these happen to be even)

☐ (Vertical) Cap height decrease 1½" (3.8cm)

☐ (Horizontal) Bicep decrease 2" (5.1cm) (Mom has very tiny arms)

☐ (Horizontal) Elbow and wrist decrease 2" (5.1cm) (this we can do in one adjustment)

What was polished in the fitting:

Mom has very rounded shoulders, which causes a large hollow space between her shoulder and bust area, and this area fluctuates. It is imperative that I put a chest pad inside her garments to pad out the shoulders and fill in this hollow spot. The shoulder darts are also key to a clean fit on the back of the garment. Wearing a bra that fits is also key to fitting her tiny frame. I pinned in her center front (apex-to-apex) area and polished up the bust darts. Mom has no bust, so any excess looks sloppy on her tiny frame. I did the usual pin in the side seams to establish the final stitching line. The size-12 pattern looked perfect on the skirt.

Fit Challenge #2

Tammie

Body description:

The most difficult thing about fitting my body is a combination of long arms and legs, and a narrow waist with larger hips. Also, as I have aged and had children and many surgeries, my abdomen has become an issue that I prefer to hide. I don't like the look of my upper arms, so I try to hide them, too.

Fun facts:

› I have been sewing since I was very young.

› I started sewing without any patterns—just draping. I think that was a great way to start.

› I have a very large sewing library.

› My nickname is "the weird sewing lady" because I like the challenge of figuring out how to make something work in sewing. Patterns are just suggestions.

Things I like to wear:

› I like all kinds of clothing.

› I like things that hide my tummy and upper arms.

› I like leggings with a long tunic, and I prefer straight-leg pants.

› My tops are all shapes and sizes.

› The jackets I like are more fitted, but are all different lengths.

› Sometimes I wear jackets and sweaters that drape.

Pattern adjustments:

☐ (Vertical) Shoulder to apex increase 2½" (6.4cm)

☐ (Vertical) Bust curve increase 1½" (3.8cm).

☐ (Vertical) Shoulder to full back increase 3½" (8.9cm) (most of her back length is toward the top)

☐ (Vertical) Back neck to waist lower back increase 2" (5.1cm)

☐ (Horizontal) Apex to apex increase 1½" (3.8cm)

☐ (Horizontal) Apex to side seam increase 2½" (6.4cm)

☐ (Horizontal) Increase front waist 3" (7.6cm)

☐ (Horizontal) Back waist increase 1½" (3.8cm)

☐ (Horizontal) Mid back increase 2" (5.1cm)

☐ (Vertical) Center front waist to hips increase 2½" (6.4cm)

☐ (Vertical) Center back waist to hips increase 3" (6.4cm)

☐ (Vertical) Cap height increase 2" (5.1cm)

☐ (Vertical) Elbow to wrist increase 2" (5.1cm)

☐ (Horizontal) Bicep increase 3" (7.6cm) (taper down the arm)

What was polished in the fitting:

I pinned in the side seams and front darts to contour around the body and determine the final shape of the stitching line. I needed to pin in a small amount down the center front of the skirt due to some excess fullness. This starts at the hem and tapers out to nothing at the waist. Finally, because I was not sure where we would like the final waist placement, I pinned horizontally across the torso to raise the waistline. I will draw these marks on the muslin and use them as a final fit pattern sloper.

Fit Challenge #3
Julie

Body description:

My biggest fitting challenge is camouflaging my mommy figure without looking like I am a busy mom of five. No mom jeans for me! I do find it hard to find clothes that fit well through all three of my challenging areas (bust, midsection and hips) while also fitting my length. I am all about comfort. I find it hard to find things fitted and flattering but comfortable.

Fun facts:

❭ I knew Joi when she was a freshman in college. My son loved to touch Joi's long hair in church, and he would even pull it.

❭ I used to make all my children's clothes so they would all match, including me. My teen girls are glad I am out of that phase now.

❭ My girls have been known to ask me to make them an outfit at 8:00PM for the next morning.

❭ I always say I sew better under pressure, but in reality I am a huge procrastinator.

Things I like to wear:

❭ I like comfy business attire.

❭ I like to look nice without giving up comfort and to be comfortable without giving up style.

❭ I like to dress up normal, everyday items like T-shirts, blazers, jeans and heels.

❭ I love skirts, blazers and shirts.

❭ I would say my style is casual dressy.

What was polished in the fitting:

The proportions look good. We pinned in the side seams and lower bust dart to conform to the body curves and determine the final stitching line. We also needed to decrease the fullness in the lower part of the skirt at the center front, so we pinned up the skirt, tapering it out to nothing at the waist. Julie has a little bit of angular excess on the side front below the bust area, so I pinned that out. We were not sure where we would like her final waistline in the adjustment increase, but decided to pin out the 1" (2.5cm) of length in question.

One interesting thing about this fit is that we do not need two waist darts in the skirt. For her body shape, the fullness created by the dart has no purpose. Julie only needs one small waist dart on the skirt, so we pinned that dart fullness down the skirt. It will be removed later.

Pattern adjustments:

☐ (Vertical) Shoulder to apex increase 1" (2.5cm)

☐ (Vertical) Bust curve increase 1½" (3.8cm)

☐ (Vertical) Underbust to waist increase 1–2" (2.5cm–5.1cm) (we weren't sure about the final waist placement, so we used a full 2" [5.1cm])

☐ (Horizontal) Apex to side seam increase 3" (7.6cm)

☐ (Horizontal) Front waist increase 6" (15.2cm)

☐ (Horizontal) Full upper back (shoulders) increase 2" (5.1cm)

☐ (Horizontal) Back waist increase 5" (12.7cm) (2" [5.1cm] will be at the center back and 3" [7.6cm] divided on each side seam)

☐ (Vertical) Waist to hip decrease 4" (10.2cm) (on her body, the full abdomen measurement is also the hip measurement)

☐ (Vertical) Waist to hips increase 3" (7.6cm)

☐ (Vertical) Cap height increase 1" (2.5cm)

☐ (Vertical) Bicep to elbow decrease 2" (5.1cm) (this is a classic example of needing to customize a pattern)

☐ (Vertical) Elbow to wrist increase 1" (2.5cm)

Fit Challenge #4

Morgan ("tween")

Body description:

I am a growing girl. I have long legs, but the upper part of my body is shorter. When I shop for clothes, many are cut too narrow or too short. It's a good thing my mom is a designer.

Fun facts:

⟩ Morgan is Joi's 10-year-old daughter.

⟩ Morgan went to the kids' sewing school at Martha Pullen School of Art Fashion and loved it.

⟩ She won a grand-prize ribbon for her first "real" sewing project at the county fair when she was 7.

⟩ Mom has to pay her a fee to model at photo shoots.

⟩ Morgan is good at photography and sets up her own photo shoots.

⟩ She is good at anything artistic.

⟩ She talks more than her mom.

Things I like to wear:

⟩ I like layers of shirts.

⟩ I love jackets with zippers.

⟩ I like clothes that are not too fitted.

⟩ I like longer skirts.

⟩ I don't like itchy, tight or short clothing.

What was polished in the fitting:

It is always fun to do dramatic changes to a pattern and see just how close a fit you can achieve simply by addressing body measurements. On this fit sample, the usual easy and expected polishing is about all that's necessary. I determined that placing the waistline just above Morgan's navel was better. I pinned the waistline seam, then I pinned in the side seams to establish the final stitching line. Because she is still developing, I pinned out some of the bust darts to create a flatter fit in the bodice. Younger girls often have a rounded front, so I also needed to pin more in from the skirt darts. Lastly, I pinned in some of the lower fullness in the skirt. These are not areas you can address in a flat pattern, so molding side seams and darts on the body is that final step to polishing the fit.

Pattern adjustments:

☐ (Vertical) Cap height decrease ½" (1.3cm)

☐ (Vertical) Bicep to elbow decrease 3" (7.6cm)

☐ (Horizontal) Bicep decrease 2" (5.1cm)

☐ (Horizontal) Elbow and wrist decrease 2" (5.1cm)

☐ (Vertical) Shoulder to apex decrease 1" (2.5cm)

☐ (Vertical) Back neck to waist decrease 1" (2.5cm) (interesting that the length decrease in the back is due to being short-waisted, while the front was higher in the torso)

☐ (Horizontal) Apex to apex decrease ½" (1.3cm)

☐ (Horizontal) Front waist increase 3" (7.6cm) (younger girls usually have a rounded tummy)

☐ (Horizontal) Back waist increase 2" (5.1cm)

☐ (Vertical) Center front waist to hips decrease 2" (5.1cm)

☐ (Vertical) Center back waist to hips decrease 1" (2.5cm) (she has a lower back hipline)

☐ (Horizontal) Center front to side seam at hips increase 1½" (3.8cm)

Morgan is begging me to make her a dress from this now. I can take this apart and use the upper part as a pattern for a dress, jacket, shirt or other garment, and the skirt can be modified to a shorter skirt with leggings or a longer skirt. I can also do a traditional slash-and-spread to make A-line designs or a gathered skirt. This pattern will allow for lots of design flexibility. This is a great method for teens and tweens when their bodies are changing and it's difficult to find clothing that fits.

Fit Challenge #5
Cheryl

Body description:

For me, the most difficult aspect of fitting garments is that my bust is large, and I'm short-waisted. I am self-conscious of that and always wear a jacket. I have always wanted to wear a sheath dress, but so far that has not worked out so well.

Fun facts:

❭ I am a 67-year-old grandmother.

❭ I have always loved fashion, so I love watching *Project Runway*.

❭ I have tried all my life to make a dress that would look nice on me, but have never accomplished that.

❭ I have enjoyed getting back into garment sewing. I like spending good money on fabric and not just making a quilt out of it.

❭ Jackets are what I love making the most.

Things I like to wear:

❭ I love long sweaters and straight-leg pants.

❭ When dressing up, I usually wear a long skirt with a jacket and boots.

❭ I like shorter skirts, too.

❭ In the summer I wear capri pants with longer tops or a T-shirt and a jacket.

Pattern adjustments:

☐ (Vertical) Shoulder to apex increase 2" (5.1cm)

☐ (Vertical) Bust curve increase 1½" (3.8cm)

☐ (Vertical) Back neck to waist increase 1½" (3.8cm)

☐ (Horizontal) Apex to apex increase 1" (2.5cm)

☐ (Horizontal) Apex to side seam increase 3" (7.6cm)

☐ (Horizontal) Front waist increase 4" (10.2cm)

☐ (Horizontal) Back waist increase 4" (10.2cm)

☐ All lower body measurements match closely enough to the pattern body measurements that no adjustments are necessary other than the waist increases

☐ (Vertical) Bicep to elbow decrease 1½" (3.8cm)

☐ (Vertical) Elbow to wrist increase 1" (2.5cm)

☐ (Horizontal) Bicep decrease 1½" (3.8cm)

What was polished in the fitting:

Cheryl always comments on how challenging it is to fit her bust. Like all our other fitting samples, we are left with minor polishing after the proportion adjustments. The side seams were pinned in to contour to the body, and the waist darts were taken in a bit. With larger bust sizes, you *want* the bust darts to contour to the body. It is much more slimming to have the shaping rather than a generic dart, so don't overlook that when fitting. I also adjusted her waist seam up slightly to create a better proportion. Cheryl did require some padding in the shoulders to smooth out the upper torso, but other than that, she was an easy fit.

Fit Challenge #6
Carol

Joi's notes:

This sample was created during one of my live classes where I taught four days of draping. They draped a design on a dress form, then used my method to adjust areas of measure to match their body. I fitted everyone in class and, even over their clothing, the fit samples looked amazing.

Body description:

I am built like a triangle, so ready-to-wear dresses never fit. When I fit the hips, the top is too big, and when I fit the top, the hips are too tight. Thus, I wear a lot of separates. Fitting pants is a challenge because my waist is 14" (35.6cm) smaller than my hips. Needless to say, before I took Joi's class, I did not have many clothes that fit well.

Fun facts:

> I have a dedicated sewing room that I use almost every day.

> I have seventeen grandchildren, and I make each girl something for Christmas, spring and their birthdays. I sew for every size you can imagine. The older girls are more challenging because the fit has to be precise.

Things I like to wear:

> I prefer simple, classic lines in my clothing, like princess seams, jackets and pants.

> I am only 5'4" (163cm) tall, so tops and jackets have to hit me right below the waist or longer to match my mid-thigh.

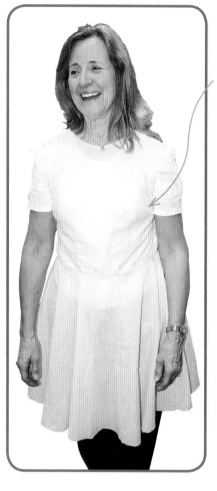

Pattern adjustment:

☐ We pinned up the shoulders.

What was polished in the fitting:

The only other polishing I would recommend would be to do some angular pinning in the lower side panels to create a smooth, wrinkle-free garment.

Comment from Carol

"I have used what I learned in your class so much! I have a granddaughter who is 4'11" (150cm) and wears a 32GG bra. Her waist is 27" (68.6cm). Being able to make a pattern to fit her has made her so happy! I used her body as a mannequin and then, because of you and your methods, I added the ease needed and got a perfect fit. She had the biggest smile on her face when she did the final fitting. Thank you so much for sharing and teaching your methods."

Patricia

Joi's notes:

Patricia is a student from one of my four-day design schools where I taught draping, followed by my pattern-fitting method. I loved working with her so much. We don't have her fit sample from class, but she was gracious enough to let us discuss her body type in this chapter. One might think she has a difficult body type to fit, but by applying a few body contouring techniques and using her measurements, we can create a garment that fits and camouflages her fit issues easily.

Body description:

The most difficult fitting problems center around my scoliosis. All of my clothes have hems at the wrong angle, and fitted clothing pulls up on my left hip. I also have narrow, uneven shoulders and am short-waisted, so fitted dresses stick out on my back. The third problem is that my hips are larger than my bust, so I need to alter there too.

Fun facts:

〉 I love to embroider.

〉 I love lace, pin tucks, shadow appliqué and all those heirloom techniques.

〉 I was once an usher for Richard Nixon when he came to Rochester, New York, while campaigning (around 1960) and was an intern for one week for Robert Kennedy.

Things I like to wear:

〉 I like to wear A-line or straight skirts.

〉 I love princess seam dresses that are fitted but not too tight.

≫ Adjusting for Spiral Curvatures

Solutions for scoliosis are also appropriate for those with a dowager's hump on the back. Measure the left and right separately and adjust points of measure accordingly to camouflage any uneven body lines. Vertical seams and darts around the neckline allow for better tailoring around those dramatic curvatures of the spine. Allow extra ease in the width areas when fitting a dowager's hump.

Pattern adjustments/body evaluation:

☐ Uneven shoulders: By contouring Patricia's left shoulder, we can raise it to match the other shoulder. Never fit to the defect when you have uneven shoulders. This is an easy fix to level out the body.

☐ Apex to apex: We might use an artificial apex point to create the illusion of where these points are on the body.

☐ Side seam waist to hips: This is a perfect example of taking this measurement on both sides of the body. Visually, we can see that one hip is dramatically higher than the other. We can raise the lower hip on her right and even out the body for lower garments.

☐ Front and back waist: Patricia is a great example of a waistline not being a harsh straight line. Her waist dips and angles in various places around the body. Her center front and center back are lower than the side seams. This is one of those cases where, when truing the side seams, I would draw the final waist on the fit sample.

☐ Arm length: It is most important to even out the shoulders when fitting the sleeves. To even out the sleeve hems, one might be just a bit longer with the other just a bit shorter to create that even illusion.

☐ By contouring the body first, it is easy to address a combination body like Patricia's and create lovely, fitted clothing that conceals the body shape. This creates a naturally shaped pattern rather than joining odd shapes, which can be difficult for even a seasoned sewist.

Fit Challenge #8

Susan

Joi's notes:

Susan was another student from one of my live classes. She learned to drape her own patterns on a standard-size dress form, then I showed her how to use my body-measuring method to change areas on that standard pattern to match her body shape and proportion. Susan created a lovely bodice pattern that was near perfect her first time out. This will be a great pattern sloper for her. She can create a dress, shirt, blouse, empire design and more all from fitting a simple princess line sloper.

Body description:

My body is a mid-50s round. I now have a round tummy that needs to be accommodated without making me look too big. I also have round upper arms.

Pattern adjustments:

☐ The apex to apex was in the perfect placement.

☐ We pinned in the princess seams just enough to remove any excess and conform to her body.

☐ The only major change was shortening the length of the bodice to create a better balance and proportion between the top and bottom of the body.

Fun facts:

⟩ I started sewing in 4-H when I was 10.

⟩ I started sewing to save money.

⟩ I resumed sewing in my mid-40s to sew doll clothes and save money.

⟩ My, how times have changed in sewing!

⟩ When I started sewing again, my good friend told me to buy fabric that I really liked when I saw it. Otherwise, it may disappear before I have a project for it. I now have cupboards full of fabric—oops!

Things I like to wear:

⟩ I like classic, tailored garments in fun colors.

⟩ My daughter likes the same, but a little edgier.

Lisa

Joi's notes:

Lisa has a challenge fitting her bust because she is blessed in this area, yet her waist is very small. She brought this fit sample to me based on my online class, and I was pretty impressed with it for a first-time pattern. After applying her body measurements, she has a great fit. This will be a nice torso sloper pattern to build some of her ballroom gown designs from, along with blouses, dresses, jackets and more.

Body description:

I have a small frame with large breasts (tatas, as my sister would say) and a very small waist. I also have long legs for my body.

Fun facts:

⟩ I first met Joi at a sewing school and have since become a Joi sewing groupie. I follow her around the U.S. and take all of her classes—she's like a rock star (okay, a sewing star)!

⟩ I sew beautiful heirloom garments and children's clothing, but I have always had trouble fitting adults. That is the reason I took Joi's class in the first place, but I learned so many other things.

⟩ I am Joi's unofficial intern.

⟩ Joi taught me how to drape and fit patterns on my body. I practice by taking measurements of other people and making garments just to see if they fit. My family is tired of the phone calls asking them to measure themselves.

⟩ I am hooked on fashion sewing.

Things I like to wear:

⟩ I love competition ballroom gowns—yes, I am a dancer!

⟩ I love dressing up.

⟩ I would wear a ball gown and diamonds every day and would be the perfect June Cleaver vacuuming in my pearls!

⟩ I love the feel of quality fabric like silk velvet, silks, alpaca and Italian wool.

⟩ I am making wool coats, blazers and jackets—a couture look inspired by Joi's trunk show. This is very different from my usual Swiss batiste and French laces.

Pattern adjustments:

☐ We polished the fit sample by pinning in the side seams and darts to conform closer to her body.

☐ With a full bust, you do not want a lot of baggy fabric underneath the "girls."

☐ Correct placement of the side bust darts is key.

☐ Even though she has a dominant curvature in the upper torso, with the right pattern proportion she is able to fit her body without tons of seams and darts.

Applying Measurements to Men's Patterns

Joi's notes:

Did I save the best for last? Or do guys only need one page because men are easier to fit or are not as particular about their clothing?

Actually, the simple answer is that I had to stay focused and not delve into an entirely different subject. But I do get questions on how to use this method on men's tailoring and garments, such as men's shirts, and how to address a husky build or longer torso. Men have obstacles in fitting just like women do. Maybe that's the subject for another book someday, but you have everything you need to apply the same method to men's patterns right here. Find an area of measure on the body and compare it to the pattern. Sure, there are some differences in the male figure, but the process is the same.

Pattern adjustments relevant to men's clothing:

☐ Arm lengths

☐ Back shoulders

☐ Center front increase for wide neck

☐ Lengthening the torso for tall sizes

☐ Horizontal increases for a husky build

☐ Upper chest

☐ Front waist

☐ Back waist

☐ Hips or seat

☐ Factor in the man's build when considering any horizontal and vertical increases or decreases: athletic, slender, stocky, pear-shaped or big-and-tall

Fun facts:

〉 Men button their shirts left over right.

〉 Larger waists look better in pleated pants.

〉 Sleeve lengths should end where the palm meets the arm.

〉 If you take the time to tailor a beautiful man's shirt, *air dry only* to prevent the fabric from shrinking.

〉 Measure a man's shirt length starting at the center back neck, across the shoulder and down the bent arm to the wrist.

〉 Shirt buttons should be between ½"–⅝" (1.3mm–1.6cm). The biggest mistake home sewists make is putting large buttons on a man's shirt.

〉 Buttonholes for a man's shirt should always be vertical except on the collar stand. (Thanks, Janet Pray of www.islandersewing.com, for your expertise in shirt fitting.)

Conclusion

Fit books always look so, well, perfect! There is always a beautifully fitted model and textbook fit issues corrected with textbook fitting solutions. While Abby, my friend and model, is darling, even she has fit issues. I hope I have presented my ideas and fitting solutions in a way that allows you to realize my method is real, flexible, fluid and customizable by targeting specific areas on the body. This is for everyone, no matter what shape or size. Fit should not create anxiety. Lose the fluff and get solutions.

In the real world, there is an unlimited combination of people and fitting needs. Yes, some textbook solutions do work for some people. More often than not, however, fitting skills and techniques need to be customized for each individual. I'm realistic when it comes to fitting. I don't want my students looking at a picture and thinking to themselves, "Hey, I'm supposed to fit that same way on myself." Every person is different, and you will have specific reasons why you do or do not do something on a particular pattern, and it may be different every time. And you know what? That's okay!

Throughout the pattern application chapters, you have learned an easy and fluid process for mastering measurements of specific areas and creating patterns that directly reflect the shape and proportion of your own unique body shape. Each area of measure has been treated as an individual pattern adjustment. As you become more comfortable, you will start to do multiple adjustments in one quick process. In Chapter 8, we walked through fitting, ease and some of those final polishing details. In Chapter 9, we reviewed through a variety of garment styles and suggested areas of measuring with pattern adjustments as well as locations of ease. Finally, we have seen real-life people and how measuring the body and adjusting specific areas truly solved their fit issues.

It has been my pleasure sharing my skills with you! Thank you for taking the time to join me in the studio.

—Joi

Remember

Fit is fluid. *It is all about problem solving, and it is okay to do something different if it works.*

Fit should be efficient. *Scale the pattern first to eliminate a majority of your fit issues.*

Not every person or garment *will need every pattern adjustment.*

Start with T-locations such as the vertical bustline and apex to apex. *Master these few adjustments, then add more as you feel confident.*

You can measure and adjust any area of any pattern *beyond what is illustrated in this book. Feel free to create your own areas of measure.*

Enjoy *garment sewing with greater success!*

Index

A

A-line gored skirt, 117
abdomen, 72
    accomodating large, 128, 129, 134
    to center front waist, 52
    to side seam, 70–71
adjustments
    to create illusions, 31, 106
    distributing evenly, 42, 95
    process, 12
    splitting up, 65
apex, 9
    to apex, 31–32
    and darts, 17
    locating, 16
    to shoulder, 16–17
    to side seam, 33–34
armholes
    polished, 108
    truing, 24–25, 47
arms, 78, 86
    bicep to elbow, 83
    biceps, 88
    combinations, 96
    elbow to wrist, 84
    elbows, 92, 95
    even distribution, 95
    horizontal measurement chart, 87
    neck to shoulder, 80
    shoulder to bicep, 81
    underarm measurements, 86, 96
    vertical measurement chart, 79
    wrists, 93
asymmetries, 10

B

back
    combination adjustments, 46
    full back to shoulder (vertical), 22
    mid, 42
    neck to waist, 23
    other adjustments, 44–45, 46–47
    upper, 40–41, 47
    vertical line to center back waist, 44, 68–69
back waist, 43, 44
ball gowns, 122
biceps, 88–89. see also arms

blouses, 114
bodices, 115
body contouring, 11
body movement, 9, 103
body types, 10, 126
    challenges with scoliosis, 133
    large abdomens, 128, 129, 134
    large bust, 131, 135
    large hips, 128, 132, 133
    long arms and legs, 128
    mom figures, 129
    narrow shoulders, 132, 133
    rounded shoulders, 127
    short-waisted, 131, 133
    small frames, 127, 135
    triangular, 132
    of tween girls, 130
boxy jacket, 113
bras. see undergarments
bust. see also apex
    adding cups, 105
    curve, 18–20
    full measurement, 30
    large sizes, 131
    saggy breasts, 11
    triple marking, 109
    uneven, 11
    to waist, 38
    to waist (vertical), 38–39, 66–67
bustline, 9

C

cap height, 81–82
cap shoulder point, 9
chest, upper, 37
coat dresses, 121
coats, 113, 119
collarbones, prominent, 90
contorting, 37
contouring, 11
    versus contorting, 37
    materials for, 11
    with padding, 105

D

darts, 17, 19
Dowager's hump, 11, 133
dress forms, 11
dresses
    ball gowns, 122

    coat, 121
    everyday, 120
    formal, 123
    princess line, 118

E

ease, 72, 74
    and fabric type, 103
    guidelines, 100
    intersecting details, 101
    little or none, 101
    and movement lines, 103
    silhouette, 102
elbow, 92, 95. see also arms

F

fashion patterns, 112
fit samples, 104, 106
    fitting, 106–109
    angular pinning, 109
    extra fabric, 109
    padding, 105
    pin fitting, 59, 107
    shoes for, 104
    undergarments, 104
fitting shell patterns, 8
foundations. see undergarments
front waist, 35–36. see also waist

G

grainlines, 39

H

hemming, 51, 52
hiplines, 50
hips
    center back to side seam, 74–75
    to center back waist (vertical), 56–57
    center front to side seam, 72–73
    to center front waist, 50–51
    curves, 59, 108
    high on one side, 11
    to side seam waist, 54–55

J
jackets, 113, 119

K
knee to center front waist, 53

L
L-slash, 37, 40, 89, 94
lower body, 48, 60. *see also* hips; waist
    horizontal combinations, 76
    horizontal measurement chart, 61
    vertical combinations, 58
    vertical measurement chart, 49

M
measuring, 9, 12, 31, 67
men's clothing, 136
mid back, 42

N
neck
    to shoulder point, 80
    to waist, 23
neckline shaping, 108

P
padding, 11, 105
pants, 116
    crotch curve template, 77
    key measurements for, 77
    "low rise" styles, 77
pattern measuring, 12
pattern sizes, 126
pin fitting, 59, 107, 109
polished fit, 13, 98, 107, 108
princess coat, 119
princess seams, 115, 118

S
scoliosis, 11, 133
seam allowances, 12
shirts, 114
shorts, 116

shoulder pads, 91, 105
shoulders
    to apex, 16–17
    to bicep, 81–82
    cap height, 81
    forward-tilting, 90, 91, 105, 108
    to full back, 22
    length, 80
    narrow, 11, 41
    uneven heights, 11, 133
    upper back measurement, 40–41
side darts, 19
side seams
    to apex, 33–34
    blending tips, 59
    to center back at hips, 74–75
    to center back waist, 64–65
    to center front abdomen, 70–71
    to center front at hips, 72–73
    to center front waist, 62–63
    truing, 27
    waist to hips, 54–55
silhouettes. *see* body types
skirts, 117
slash-and-spread ttechnique, 12
sleeve caps
    adjustments, 25
    back upper half cap, 90–91
    cap height, 81–82
    cap shoulder point, 9
    ease, 82
sleeves, 97, 108. *see also* arms
    contouring for fullness, 96
    front and back comparison, 86
    lengthening or shortening, 84, 85
supplies, 88

T
tools, 8
torso, 14, 28. *see also* back; waist
    horizontal combination adjustments, 46
    horizontal measurement chart, 29
    vertical combination adjustments, 26
    vertical measurement chart, 15
truing, 12

armholes, 24–25
side seams, 27

U
underarms, 86, 96
underbust
    full measurement, 30
    to waist, 21
undergarments, 10, 104, 105
upper back, 40–41, 47
upper chest, 37

V
vertical bustline, 38, 66

W
waist
    to back neck, 23
    back waist, 43
    center back to back vertical line, 68–69
    center back to hips, 56–57
    center back to side seams, 64–65
    center front to abdomen, 52
    center front to hips, 50–51
    center front to knee, 53
    center front to lower vertical bustline, 38–39, 66–67
    center front to side seam, 62–63
    front waist, 35–36
    full measurement, 30
    side to hips, 54–55
    to underbust, 21
wrists, 93–94. *see also* arms

Resources

Online Classes

If you enjoyed this book, you'll like Joi's online classes on the same fitting methods (visit www.designerjoi.com to sign up):

〉Fast-Track Fitting with Joi Mahon
〉Fast-Track Fitting in the Details with Joi Mahon

Other resources

Oak tag sheets available at www.amazon.com.

Bra pads available at www.brazabra.com.

Sewing supplies available at www.wawak.com or your local craft store.

Special Thanks

I want to offer a special thank-you to Dr. Carolyn Kundel, my pattern-making professor and now dear friend. It was so wonderful to study under you and gain your expertise, and I value all the extra projects and independent studies you mentored me in. I could not have studied under anyone better. You are like family. P.S.—I still have all my class projects and my half-scale binder of hundreds of patterns created in class. Flat pattern was my favorite class! (Dr. Kundel's book is the best reference for flat pattern, and you may share her expertise by studying **Pattern Making by the Flat-Pattern Method, 8th edition** by Norma R. Hollen and Carolyn J. Kundel).

I also want to give a special thanks to Linda Rogers, the most talented tailor and alteration specialist I have ever met. Thanks for hiring me as an eager fourteen-year-old aspiring sewist and giving me years of opportunities to fit any body type you can imagine: men, women, children, young, old, tall, short, big and small. That was a valuable experience for building my skills, and I am grateful.

Design Aids

For these and other high-quality design tools and items that I offer my students in live classes, visit www.designerjoi.com:

〉25yd (22.9m) bolts of 45"/60" (1.1m/1.5m)-wide, high-quality draping and pattern-making muslin
〉PGM industrial dress forms (custom-color options available)
〉Tailoring pads, body contour padding and shapers, draping tape, patternmaking rulers and more
〉Technical draping fabric with grid
〉Draping tape, pattern-making rulers
〉Designer Joi Pattern Adjustment Stickers, Pattern Template Rulers and Embroidery Collection
〉Designer Joi Patterns (McCall Pattern Company)

Dedication

I dedicate this book to my grandmother, Margaret Vredenburgh, who would have loved this and always showed interest in my sewing, even at a very young age; and to all my family, friends and students who still show interest in something I am so passionate about.

Acknowledgments

One person does not achieve something on her own. It takes a dream and a team.

First, I want to thank the good Lord, who is creative himself. I am thankful for being allowed to be a creative person. It is a gift that I feel obligated to use for good and to my fullest potential. I don't have to prove myself to anyone if I am always doing my best.

To my hubby for putting up with my crazy ambition and daily quote of "Hey, I have another idea."

To my daughter, Morgan, for always telling me, "Mom you are the best designer ever," to which I reply, "You can have a pony."

To my little man, Sammy, who keeps me on my toes and plays trains and trucks on my computer when I am trying to type. You keep priorities in perspective.

To my mom and dad, my in-laws and my sister (the true writing talent in the family) for your interest and support.

To Janet Pray, founder of the American Sewing Expo, and Steve Jeffery, president of Baby Lock USA, for being wonderful professional mentors, believing in me and letting me run with my design ideas.

To Abby, my amazing model and friend; your personality shines when you model, and we always have the best time.

To Roxanne, for being so creative and designing hair styles for all my photo shoots.

To Andrea, for being a fabulous photographer. You really get my ideas and even let me help myself to your props and boss people around during photo shoots. We make a great team!

To Chuck Islander, for your editing eye and technical photography advice and for helping me develop the measurement charts.

Thank you to all my Real People volunteers. Your willingness to be candid about your fit issues brings this book full circle and allows for practical real-life application.

Thank you to Vogue Patterns for use of the Misses' Fitting Shell 1004 to illustrate my technique.

Thank you to SnapFashun.com for use of your technical flats in Chapter 9. I was trained in SnapFashun years ago. You are a great professional resource, and it was exciting to use it in this book.

Thank you to Baby Lock Sewing Machines for believing in all my design creativity and helping me bring my ideas to sewists everywhere.

Thank you to F+W Media: Amelia for helping to promote my book idea, Noel for being such a great editor, and all of those who had a part in making this happen. It was a team effort.

Most important, thank you to my readers, students and sewing friends for their interest in my work. I hope I inspire others and that you receive as much fulfillment in creativity as I do.

a content + ecommerce company

www.fwmedia.com

18 17   5 4

Distributed in Canada by Fraser Direct
100 Armstrong Avenue
Georgetown, ON, Canada L7G 5S4
Tel: (905) 877-4411

Distributed in the U.K. and Europe by F+W MEDIA
INTERNATIONAL
Brunel House, Newton Abbot, Devon, TQ12 4PU, England
Tel: (+44) 1626 323200, Fax: (+44) 1626 323319
Email: postmaster@davidandcharles.co.uk

Distributed in Australia by Capricorn Link
P.O. Box 704, S. Windsor NSW, 2756 Australia
Tel: (02) 4560 1600, Fax: (02) 4577 5288
Email: books@capricornlink.com.au

ISBN-13: 978-1-4402-3961-8
ISBN-10: 1-4402-3961-4
SRN: U9383

Metric Conversion Chart

to convert	to	multiply by
Inches	Centimeters	2.54
Centimeters	Inches	0.4
Feet	Centimeters	30.5
Centimeters	Feet	0.03
Yards	Meters	0.9
Meters	Yards	1.1

Projects have been designed and created using imperial measurements and, although metric measurements have been provided, it
is important to stick to using either imperial or metric throughout, as
discrepancies can occur.

Edited by **Noel Rivera**

Interior book design by **Elyse Schwanke**

Cover design by **Kelly Pace**

Photography by **Andrea Zenor, Bobier Photography**

Illustrations by **SnapFashun.com**

Styling by **Roxanne Raveling**

Production coordinated by **Greg Nock**

About the Author

Fashion designer **Joi Mahon** has a long background in fitting just about every body type and issue imaginable. Like many sewists, Joi discovered a love of sewing at a very young age. She took her one and only sewing lesson in sixth grade and instantly found her gift. In high school, she was already working for a tailor, learning men's tailoring, alterations and bridal gown design, and fitting men, women, children, young, old, big, small and so on. She taught her first sewing class when she was thirteen to other junior high and high school students and won numerous awards for her sewing. She studied fashion design and product development at Iowa State University and was the student up every Friday night, *not* partying, but designing clothing in her dorm room.

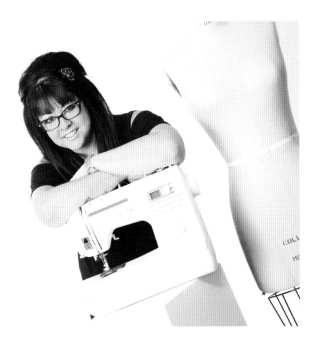

She always knew she would start her own business and, the week after graduating top in her class, she leased office space and has never had a lack of customers. Joi designs custom clothing for clients all over the U.S., many of whom she never sees in person. She had a college professor once ask how she does this with such accuracy, and, well, this book is her trade secret.

Joi owns a patent on a clothing design; won the Passion for Fashion competition (like an episode of *Project Runway*) at the American Sewing Expo; is a product developer, published author, embroidery and pattern designer; and has the honor of being sponsored by Baby Lock Sewing Machines and teaching their Love of Fashion programs.

Joi travels around the country to various sewing and fashion events, teaching her skills and experience. While traveling, Joi hears over and over again how sewists buy every fit book and take every class, and they still have problems with fit. Joi does not teach traditional methods because, often, they do not provide the solutions sewists are looking for. Joi teaches methods she uses in her studio every day that work. Joi has been sewing professionally since she was fifteen, over half her life, and she hopes you will enjoy this book and gain enjoyment and practical ease in your sewing and fit from her firsthand experience. For more about Joi's current happenings and offerings, visit www.designerjoi.com.

Connect — Inspire — Create

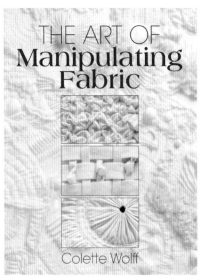

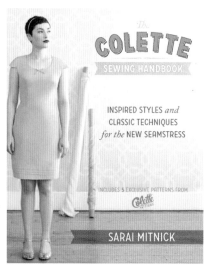

The Art of Manipulating Fabric

Colette Wolff

Working from the simplest possible form—a flat piece of cloth and a threaded needle—Colette Wolff categorizes all major dimensional techniques, show how they are related, and give examples of variations both traditional and modern. The result is an encyclopedia of techniques that resurfaces, reshapes, restructures and reconstructs fabric. This book provides more than 350 diagrams that support the extensive how-tos, organized into broad general categories, then specific sub-techniques.

Pattern Fitting with Confidence

Nancy Zieman

Nancy Zieman's pattern fitting approach is easy—no cutting, slashing, tucking or pinching—just logical and easy pivot-and-slide techniques, providing a painless method to follow that results in a garment that is comfortable and attractive. Once you learn Nancy's techniques for fitting, you will find it easy to make every garment you sew fit your size and shape. Multiple fitting charts are included in the book, as well as an index for locating technical information at a glance.

The Colette Sewing Handbook

Sarai Mitnick

Five simple fundamentals can help you perfect any sewing project: a thoughtful plan, a precise pattern, a fantastic fit, a beautiful fabric, and a fine finish. With these five core ideas, *The Colette Sewing Handbook* shows you how to start sewing the wardrobe of your dreams. This book Includes five beautiful patterns for modern classic pieces, including a scalloped-hem skirt, flutter-sleeve blouse, sweetheart neck sheath dress, asymmetrical flounce dress, and a lined dress with gathered sleeves.

For more sewing books and products, check out sewdaily.com